The
Quotable
Athlete

The Quotable Athlete

Words of Wisdom
from Michael Jordan, Mia Hamm,
Bonnie Blair, Wayne Gretzky,
Joe Thiesman, and More

MIKE MCGOVERN
SUSAN SHELLY

McGraw-Hill

New York   San Francisco   Washington, D.C.   Auckland   Bogotá
Caracas   Lisbon   London   Madrid   Mexico City   Milan
Montreal   New Delhi   San Juan   Singapore
Sydney   Tokyo   Toronto

McGraw-Hill

A Division of The **McGraw·Hill** Companies

1 2 3 4 5 6 7 8 9 0   DOC/DOC   0 9 8 7 6 5 4 3 2 1 0

ISBN 0-07-136062-X

Printed and bound by R. R. Donnelley & Sons Company.

McGraw-Hill books are available at special quantity discounts to use as pre-
miums and sales promotions, or for use in corporate training programs. For
more information, please write to the Director of Special Sales, Professional
Publishing, McGraw-Hill, Two Penn Plaza, New York, NY 10121-2298. Or
contact your local bookstore.

This publication is designed to provide accurate and authoritative information
in regard to the subject matter covered. It is sold with the understanding that
neither the author nor the publisher is engaged in rendering legal, accounting,
or other professional service. If legal advice or other expert assistance is
required, the services of a competent professional person should be sought.
*—From a Declaration of Principles jointly adopted by a Committee of the
American Bar Association and a Committee of Publishers.*

This book is printed on recycled, acid-free paper containing a
minimum of 50% recycled, de-inked fiber.

This book is dedicated to all athletes—from high-profile professionals to the kids who play their hearts out on athletic fields all across the country. And, to our own athletes, Sara and Ryan McGovern, who have generated some pretty interesting quotes of their own.

Contents

⁓ *Introduction* ⁓

You've probably seen and heard this scenario play out more than a few times. The game is over and it was thrilling and surprising and rife with drama. You're already late for an appointment, but you can't pull yourself away from the television, because you've just got to hear what the coach and the star player have to say.

So finally, after the seemingly endless string of commercials has ended, the broadcasters in the booth throw it down to the reporter in the locker room.

"Coach, your team played with a lot of heart, despite trailing by 10 points with four minutes to play. Do you think this game will be a turning point in your season?"

"Well, you know, I hate to look too far ahead. All I'd like to say is it was a great win and we'll just go forward from here, taking one game at a time and doing our best to play hard and stay focused."

"Let's bring in tonight's hero, Spanky Spunkmeyer. Spanky, how did you manage to play so well, scoring 43 points, with a sprained ankle and a 103-degree fever? Where did you find the will?"

"Well, I always try to play as hard as I can, because every game is important."

For that, you made yourself late?

It's a fact. Some coaches and athletes speak in cliches, with a tendency to state the obvious. Sometimes, you wonder why the media bother to stick a microphone in sports figures' faces or write down their pronouncements on a notepad.

But thankfully, not all sports figures opt for the bland and the boring when it comes to answering questions or dispensing their opinions. Thankfully, there are athletes and coaches who are witty and wise, insightful and entertaining, thoughtful and thought-provoking.

The Quotable Athlete showcases sports figures with something to say and an interesting way to say it on a variety of topics—from adversity to attitude, from respect to racism, from swearing to sportsmanship, from money to motivation.

Some of those quoted will be well known icons in their sport; others will be relatively anonymous, known only to their family and friends. But the common denominator is their words and the impact they have.

Because athletes are held up as celebrities in our sports-obsessed society, they are constantly in the public eye. We react with great interest not only to their athletic victories and defeats but also to their personal successes and failures. Athletes are closely watched and extensively interviewed, and their thoughts and observations are widely debated and discussed.

The book includes quotes from athletes of nearly every major endeavor, from professional and college football, to women's soccer, to auto racing, to minor league baseball.

You'll find quotes from athletes who are men and women, professional and amateur, living and dead, who are just starting their careers, and who are long retired and reflecting upon their accomplishments. Although some of the quotes in the book are well known and have been widely circulated, others are relatively little known. But it's not the speaker's celebrity that's important, it's what the speaker has to say.

A great quote might be from Yogi Berra: "Baseball is 90 percent mental. The other half is physical"; Charles Barkley: "My initial response was to sue her for defamation of character, but then I realized that I had no character"; Vince Lombardi: "Individual commitment to a group effort—that is what makes a team work, a company work, a society work, a civilization work"; Arnold Palmer: "Golf takes more mental energy, more concentration, more determination than any other sport ever invented"; or Michael Jordan: "If you run into a wall, don't turn around and give up. Figure out how to climb it, go through it, or work around it."

Or maybe an athlete you've never heard of has said something that proves you don't have to be famous to be quotable. Deontey Kenner, a quarterback for the University of Cincinnati, isn't high profile, but his sentiments regarding his family and his determination to earn his degree still ring true: "My dream is to be able to pay back my mother and grandmother for all the sacrifices they've made for me. If I can do that with the NFL, that's great, but if I can't I want to make sure I can take care of them through my work. It might take me a little longer, but I'll do it."

The Quotable Athlete is a collection to learn from and to enjoy. It proves that athletes do indeed have something to say.

 Accomplishment

I was in Cooperstown the day Satchel Paige was inducted, and I stayed awake almost all that night thinking about it. It's something you never had any dream you'd ever see. Like men walking on the moon. I always wanted to go up there to Cooperstown. You felt like you had a reason, because it's the home of baseball, but you didn't have a special reason. We never thought we'd get in the Hall of Fame. We thought the way we were playing was the way it was going to continue. I never had any dream it would come. But that night I felt like I was part of it at last.

> BUCK LEONARD,
> Negro League Star and Hall of Famer,
> as quoted in *Everything You Always Wanted to Know About
> Sports and Didn't Know Where to Ask*
> by Mickey Herskowitz and Steve Perkins, 1977

I was a dirt bag. Now I'm an All-Pro.

> JIM BURT,
> New York Giants tackle,
> on winning the team's first NFC championship since 1956,
> as quoted in *True Blue: From Giants to Supermen*
> by Eric Pooley, 1987

 Adversity

You cannot serve water with a pitchfork.

> FRANK LUCCHESI,
> former manager of the Texas Rangers,
> referring to the difficulty of winning with a bad team,
> as quoted in *Sports Illustrated*, May 17, 1976

In a crisis, don't hide behind anything or anybody. They're going to find you anyway.

> ―PAUL "BEAR" BRYANT,
>> legendary University of Alabama football coach,
>> in *The Book of Football Wisdom*, edited by Criswell Freeman,
>> 1996

I had to fight all my life to survive. They were all against me . . . but I beat the bastards and left them in the ditch.

> ―TY COBB,
>> baseball player, manager, and legendary Hall of Famer,
>> as quoted in *Baseball: The Early Years* by Harold Seymour,
>> 1960

With adversity came maturity. No situation scares me now.

> ―JEFF BLAKE,
>> quarterback,
>> reflecting on his six seasons with the Cincinnati Bengals after
>> he was signed by the New Orleans Saints,
>> as quoted in *Sports Illustrated*, February 21, 2000

I'll take the two-shot penalty, but I'll be damned if I'm going to play the ball where it lies.

> ―ELAINE JOHNSON,
>> professional golfer,
>> after her ball bounced off a tree and landed in her bra,
>> as quoted in *Golfers on Golf*, edited by Downs MacRury,
>> 1997

Jackie, we've got no army. There's virtually nobody on our side. No owners, no umpires, very few newspapermen. And I'm afraid that many fans may be hostile. We'll be in a tough position. We can win only if we can convince the world that I'm doing this because you're a great ballplayer, a fine gentleman.

> ―BRANCH RICKEY,
>> major league baseball innovator and president-general man-
>> ager of the Brooklyn Dodgers, who integrated professional
>> baseball in 1947 by bringing up Jackie Robinson,
>> referring to Robinson's anticipated reception,
>> as quoted in *Giants of Baseball* by Bill Gutman, 1975

In life, you'll get your back up against the wall many times. You might as well get used to it.

➤ PAUL "BEAR" BRYANT,
  legendary University of Alabama football coach,
  in *The Book of Football Wisdom*, edited by Criswell Freeman,
  1996

The weather's cold, my club stinks, we can't win, my knees are killing me, I'm off my diet, I can't putt anymore, my wife's nagging me. Other than that, life's great.

➤ DON ZIMMER,
  former manager of the Chicago Cubs,
  as quoted in the *Boston Globe*, April 29, 1990

I knew we were in for a long season when we lined up for the national anthem on opening day and one of my players said, "Every time I hear that song I have a bad game."

➤ JIM LEYLAND,
  former manager of the Pittsburgh Pirates,
  as quoted in *USA Today*, July 21, 1989

It's like riding a bike on the freeway with cars coming at you.

➤ CHRIS MILLER,
  Denver Broncos quarterback,
  when asked if rejoining the National Football League after a
    three-year layoff was like getting back on a bicycle

People don't seem to understand that it's a damn war out there.

➤ JIMMY CONNORS,
  Hall of Fame tennis player,
  in *Winning is Everything and Other American Myths* by
    Thomas Tutko and William Bruns, 1976

Sooner or later . . . you are going to be looking at God saying, "We're going to be lucky if we get out of here." Your life is going to be in front of you and then you are going to realize that you'd rather be grocery shopping.

➤ ED BARRY,
  rock climber,
  as quoted in *Newsweek*, October 1, 1984

Advice

Don't cuss. Don't argue with the officials. And don't lose the game.

— JOHN HEISMAN,
legendary college football coach and namesake of the Heisman Trophy, who is credited with legalizing the forward pass and originating the center snap and the count signals of the quarterback,
as quoted in *The Book of Football Wisdom*, edited by Criswell Freeman, 1996

Just do what you do best.

— RED AUERBACH,
legendary Hall of Fame basketball coach who led the Boston Celtics to nine NBA championships—winning 1037 games against 548 losses,
as quoted in *The Ultimate Success Quotations Library*, Cyber Nation International, Inc., Reno, NV, 1997

When you're on the sleeper at night, take your pocketbook and put it in a sock under your pillow. That way, the next morning you won't forget your pocketbook, 'cause you're looking for your sock.

— FRANK "PING" BODIE,
professional baseball player,
giving advice to Yankee rookie George Halas in 1919

I'm a tough competitor, no doubt about that, but I wouldn't say I am confrontational at all. You have to really get me steamed for a confrontation, and that hasn't happened yet. I think that comes from the slow pace of growing up in the South. My grandparents used to always say, "Think before you act, and be in control at all times." I always remembered that.

— MICHAEL JORDAN,
former NBA superstar for the Chicago Bulls,
referring to accusations that he was confrontational

Take no thought of who is right or wrong or who is better than. Be not for or against.

— BRUCE LEE,
martial arts expert,
in *The Ultimate Success Quotations Library*, Cyber Nation
International, Inc., Reno, NV, 1997

Don't give advice unless you're asked.

— AMY ALCOTT,
Hall of Fame golfer,
as quoted in *The Golfer's Book of Wisdom*, edited by Criswell
Freeman, 1995

If I had to cram all my tournament experience into one sentence, I would say, "Don't give up and don't let up!"

— TONY LEMA,
professional golfer who was killed in a plane crash in 1966,
as quoted in *The Golfer's Book of Wisdom*, edited by Criswell
Freeman, 1995

No matter how many errors you make, no matter how many times you strike out, keep hustling. That way you'll at least look like a ballplayer.

— TONY KUBEK, SR.,
to his son, New York Yankees rookie shortstop Tony Kubek, Jr.,
in 1957

If you really want to advise me, do it on Saturday afternoon between 1 and 4 o'clock. And you've got 25 seconds to do it, between plays. Not on Monday. I know the right thing to do on Monday.

— ALEX AGASE,
former assistant football coach at the University of Michigan,
as quoted in *Fortune*, May 13, 1985

Age, Aging, and Longevity

When you're planning to live to one hundred, it's [turning fifty] only half-time.

➤ JOE NAMATH,
   legendary Hall of Fame quarterback,
   as quoted in the *New York Times*, January 29, 1994

Most people my age are dead at the present time.

➤ CASEY STENGEL,
   baseball player and manager of the New York Yankees and the New York Mets,
   as quoted in the Ken Burns television series *Baseball*, part IV, 1994

Everybody on that team is dead but me. I guess I didn't get on base as often as the rest of them did. Those fellas tired themselves out.

➤ MARK KOENIG,
   the last surviving member of the 1927 New York Yankees, one of the best teams of all-time,
   as quoted at age 87 by the *San Francisco Chronicle*, July 4, 1990

Forty was my worst birthday. I thought that's when you get to the end. But you change as you go on. I have as much fun now as I had then. I'm quite a showoff and people make much more of you at 80 running the marathon than they do when you're 50. At 80 you can be peculiar and say strange things and get away with so much more!

➤ LOIS SCHIEFFELIN,
   a runner from New York City, who at age 80 ran the New York Marathon in 6 hours, 32 minutes, and 6 seconds—
   a personal best—
   as quoted in *December Champions* by Bob Darden and W.R. Spence, M.D., 1993

I've taken the physical strengthening of my body seriously. Before this stage, I had my youth to live off and rely upon. Now it's not quite the same. As you grow older, the body starts giving you signals that you've got to listen to and do things that are correct. I just feel that physically I've got to be in the best shape possible to be able to do my job.

　　◆—MICHAEL JORDAN,
　　　　former NBA superstar with the Chicago Bulls,
　　　　talking about keeping in shape as he ages,
　　　　as quoted in *Michael Jordan Speaks* by Janet Lowe, 1999

As men get older, the toys get more expensive.

　　◆—MARVIN DAVIS,
　　　　former owner of the Oakland Athletics,
　　　　on the purchase of a team for an estimated $12 million,
　　　　as quoted in various news summaries, December 13, 1979

If you live long enough, lots of nice things happen.

　　◆—GEORGE HALAS,
　　　　legendary coach of the Chicago Bears and a charter member
　　　　　　of the National Football League Hall of Fame,
　　　　as quoted in *The Book of Football Wisdom*, edited by Criswell
　　　　　　Freeman, 1996; Halas lived to be 88 years old

You get smart only when you begin getting old.

　　◆—ALLIE "THE CHIEF" REYNOLDS,
　　　　professional baseball player,
　　　　widely quoted

How old would you be if you didn't know how old you was?

　　◆—SATCHEL PAIGE,
　　　　Hall of Fame pitcher in the Negro baseball league,
　　　　attributed

At my age, I'm just happy to be named the greatest living anything.

　　◆—JOE DiMAGGIO,
　　　　legendary New York Yankees outfielder and Hall of Famer,
　　　　as he was named baseball's "greatest living player" at age 66

I'll never make the mistake of being 70 again.

➤ CASEY STENGEL,
    baseball player and manager of the New York Yankees and
      New York Mets,
    remarking to the press after being fired as manager of the
      New York Yankees in 1960

Alcohol and Alcoholism

There is a distinct lack of concern on the part of management. It's
paranoia on their part. They want to keep it quiet and out of the
newspapers. They want you to believe that nothing like this could
happen in their organization.

➤ DON NEWCOMBE
    of the Brooklyn Dodgers, one of the best hitting pitchers of all
      time, who admitted that a problem with alcohol shortened
      his career,
    referring to organized baseball's attitude toward alcoholism

Stay busy, get plenty of exercise, and don't drink too much. Then
again, don't drink too little.

➤ HERMAN "JACKRABBIT" SMITH-JOHANNSEN,
    103-year-old Canadian cross-country skier, sharing his secrets
      to longevity,
    as quoted in *Sportswit* by Lee Green, 1984

 *Anger*

Anger has no place on the course.

— SANDRA PALMER,
professional golfer,
as quoted in *Golfers on Golf*, edited by Downs MacRury, 1997

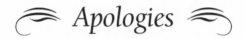 *Apologies*

I want to sincerely apologize to the people of New York and to the fans of the New York Yankees everywhere for the performance of the Yankee team in the World Series. I also want to assure you that we will be at work immediately to prepare for 1982.

— GEORGE STEINBRENNER,
controversial owner of the New York Yankees,
in a press release after the Yankees lost the 1981 World Series

The only correct actions are those that demand no explanation and no apology.

— RED AUERBACH,
legendary Hall of Fame basketball coach, who led the Boston
Celtics to nine NBA championships—winning 1037 games
against 548 losses,
from *The Ultimate Success Quotations Library*, Cyber Nation
International, Inc., Reno, NV, 1997

Athletes

It's really impossible for athletes to grow up. On the one hand, you're a child, still playing a game. But on the other hand, you're a superhuman hero that everyone dreams of being. No wonder we have such a hard time understanding who we are.

> —Billie Jean King,
> **Hall of Fame tennis player and champion for women's rights,**
> **from an Internet collection of quotations**

Now these young athletes have one more thing to deal with as they pursue excellence in sports.

> —Peggy Fleming,
> **former champion figure skater,**
> **after skater Nancy Kerrigan was attacked and her knee**
> **injured before the 1994 U.S. Nationals,**
> **as quoted in *Born to Skate: The Michelle Kwan Story* by**
> **Edward Z. Epstein, 1997**

Attitude

A bad attitude is worse than a bad swing.

> —Payne Stewart,
> **professional golfer and two-time U.S. Open champion who**
> **was killed in a plane crash in October 1999,**
> **as quoted in *Golfers on Golf*, edited by Downs MacRury, 1997**

When someone tells me there is only one way to do things, it always lights a fire under my butt. My instant reaction is, "I'm gonna prove you wrong."

> —Picabo Street,
> **Olympic gold medalist and world champion skier,**
> **as quoted in *Get Lost Adventure Magazine***

I hope, when I stop, people will think that somehow I made a difference.

— MARTINA NAVRATILOVA,
   Hall of Fame tennis player,
   as quoted in the *International Herald Tribune*, July 22, 1986

People can enjoy life. I don't believe in worrying, and I don't believe in losing your temper, because you're the only one that suffers from it! Things like that are important. You've got to love people at all levels and all ages. I think the one reason I've been fortunate is that I inherited that sort of disposition. My parents didn't get all worked up about things. I didn't go to bed at night worrying about something. If I couldn't do something at night, I'd wait until the next morning. And I feel strongly about that: you can't worry about what's going to happen. Wait and see what's going to happen.

— EUGENE L. SHIRK,
   former cross-country coach at Albright College in Reading,
      Pennsylvania, who at age 91 was the oldest college coach in
      any sport in the country,
   as quoted in *December Champions* by Bob Darden and W.R.
      Spence, M.D., 1993

The trouble with being number one in the world—in anything—is that it takes a certain mentality to attain that position, and that is something of a driving, perfectionist attitude, so that once you do achieve number one, you don't relax and enjoy it.

— BILLIE JEAN KING,
   Hall of Fame tennis player and champion for women's rights,
   from her book *Billie Jean*, 1982

Life was good to me. I had a great wife, good kids, money, my own health—and I'm lonely and bored.

— O.J. SIMPSON,
   Heisman Trophy winner and Hall of Fame football player,
      who in 1995 was accused of killing his wife, Nicole Brown
      Simpson, and her friend, Ron Goldman,
   as quoted in *The Speaker's Electronic Reference Collection*,
      AApex Software, 1994

 *Baseball*

There's three things you can do in a baseball game— you can win, you can lose, or it can rain.

> ⟿CASEY STENGEL,
>> baseball player and former manager of the New York Yankees and New York Mets,
>> as quoted in *The Guinness Dictionary of Sports Quotations* by Colin Jarman, 1990

There is always something you have to work on in baseball. You never have control of the situation. The pitcher does.

> ⟿DEION SANDERS,
>> All-Pro cornerback for the San Francisco 49ers and Dallas Cowboys, who also played major league baseball,
>> referring to why he thinks football is easier than baseball,
>> as quoted in *USA Today*, July 28, 1989

Baseball was mighty and exciting to me, but there is no blinking at the fact that at the time, the game was thought, by solid sensible people, to be only one degree above grand larceny, arson, and mayhem.

> ⟿CONNIE MACK,
>> legendary manager of the Philadelphia Athletics,
>> talking about how baseball was viewed during the 1880s,
>> as quoted in *The Giants of the Polo Grounds* by Noel Hynd, 1988

My sense is, in the end, most everybody will do what they think is best for the game and not their selfish proprietary interest.

> ⟿JERRY McMORRIS,
>> owner of the Colorado Rockies,
>> referring to players and owners acting fiscally responsible,
>> as quoted in the *Chicago Tribune*, January 16, 2000

Baseball is a public trust. Players turn over, owners turn over and certain commissions turn over. But baseball goes on.

> ⟿PETER UEBERROTH,
>> former commissioner of major league baseball,
>> as quoted in the *New York Times*, August 9, 1985

Baseball is a peculiar profession, possibly the only one which capitalized a boyhood pleasure, unfits the athlete for another career, keeps him young in mind and spirit, and then rejects him as too old before he has yet attained the prime of life.

    —GERALD BEAUMONT,
        early twentieth century journalist,
        as quoted in *Baseball's Greatest Quotations* **Paul Dickson, 1991**

I don't like comparisons with football. Baseball is an entirely different game. You can watch a tight, well-played football game, but it isn't exciting if the stadium is empty. The violence on the field must bounce off a lot of people. But you can go to the ballpark on a quiet Tuesday afternoon with only a few thousand people in the place and thoroughly enjoy a one-sided game. Baseball has an aesthetic, intellectual appeal found in no other team sport.

    —BOWIE KUHN,
        former commissioner of major league baseball,
        as quoted in *TV Guide,* **October 10, 1970**

There are only five things you can do in baseball—run, throw, catch, hit and hit with power.

    —LEO DUROCHER,
        Hall of Fame manager of the Brooklyn Dodgers and New York
            Giants,
        as quoted in *Time,* **July 16, 1973**

Baseball was, is and always will be to me the best game in the world.

    —BABE RUTH,
        legendary Hall of Fame baseball player,
        as quoted in *The Babe Ruth Story* **by Babe Ruth, as told to Bob**
            Consadine, 1948

Baseball is the champ of them all. Like somebody said, the pay is good and the hours are short.

    —YOGI BERRA,
        player, coach, manager, and a member of the Baseball Hall of
            Fame,
        as quoted in *The Sporting News,* **November 21, 1951**

This game has taken a lot of guys over the years, who would have had to work in factories and gas stations, and made them prominent people. I only had a high school education and, believe me, I had to cheat to get that. There isn't a college in the world that would have me. And yet in this business you can walk into a room with millionaires, doctors, professional people and get more attention than they get. I don't know any other business where you can do that.

➤ SPARKY ANDERSON,
   former manager of the Cincinnati Reds and Detroit Tigers, the
      first to win 100 games in a season and the World Series in
      both major leagues,
   as quoted in the *Los Angeles Times*, December 26, 1975

Basketball

There's nothing like playing basketball. I can sit there and run on the treadmill a couple miles and run lines, but it's nothing like playing in a game.

➤ SEAN ELLIOTT,
   San Antonio Spurs forward,
   referring to his desire to return to the game after a kidney
      transplant six months earlier,
   as quoted in the *Fort Worth Star-Telegram*, January 16, 2000

The game is my wife. It demands loyalty and responsibility, and it gives me back fulfillment and peace.

➤ MICHAEL JORDAN,
   former NBA superstar for the Chicago Bulls,
   as quoted in *Newsweek*, January 5, 1987

Believing

I don't even think you know how great you really are. I believe in you.

— St. Louis Rams coach DICK VERMEIL,
    encouraging his team before its January 16 National Football
      Conference divisional playoff game against the Minnesota
      Vikings in January 2000

Sometimes the biggest problem is in your head. You've got to believe you can play a shot instead of wondering where your next bad shot is coming from.

— JACK NICKLAUS,
    Hall of Fame golfer and winner of 20 major championships,
    in *The Golfer's Book of Wisdom*, edited by Criswell Freeman,
      1995

Believe deep down in your heart that you're destined to do great things.

— JOE PATERNO,
    head football coach at Penn State since 1966,
    as quoted in *The Book of Football Wisdom*, edited by Criswell
      Freeman, 1996

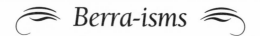

Berra-isms

(YOGI BERRA, baseball player, coach, manager and Hall of Famer is famous for quotes that have become known as Berra-isms or Yogi-isms. Several are listed below.)

A nickel ain't worth a dime anymore.

— As quoted in *Baseball Digest*, June 1987

Anybody who can't tell the difference between a ball hitting wood and ball hitting concrete must be blind.

➤ Said during an argument with an umpire,
as quoted in *Sports Illustrated*, April 30, 1979

I usually take a two-hour nap, from one o'clock to four.

➤ When asked what he normally did on the day before a night game,
from *The Wit and Wisdom of Yogi Berra* by Phil Pepe

I wish I had an answer to that because I'm getting tired of answering that question.

➤ When asked about the poor record of his 1984 Yankees team,
as quoted *in Sports Illustrated*, June 11, 1984

Why buy good luggage? You only use it when you travel.

➤ As quoted in *Yogi: It Ain't Over...* by Yogi Berra, with Tim Thorton and Tom Horton (contributor), 1997

We made too many wrong mistakes.

➤ Explaining why his Yankees team lost the 1960 World Series to the Pittsburgh Pirates

You'd better make it four. I don't think I can eat six pieces.

➤ When asked whether he wanted his pizza cut into four or six pieces

If you can't imitate him, don't copy him.

➤ Responding to a player who told Berra he liked to crowd the plate like Frank Robinson,
as quoted in *Baseball Digest*, August 1969

Baseball is 90 percent mental. The other half is physical.

➤ As quoted in *Yogi: It Ain't Over . . . . . .* by Yogi Berra, with Tim Thorton and Tom Horton, (contributor), 1997

I really didn't say everything I said.

➤ As quoted in *The Sporting News*, March 17, 1986

 *Betting*

I bet five thousand dollars on them Harvards. But the Yales win it. I'm off that football business, too.

— BABE RUTH,
 legendary Hall of Fame baseball player,
 explaining a football bet to renowned sportswriter Grantland
 Rice,
 as quoted in Rice's book, *The Tumult and the Shouting*,
 1954

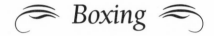 *Boxing*

There ain't nothing like being in the corner, and the trainer is whispering in your ear and another guy is putting in your mouthpiece. Five seconds to go, then boom! The bell. It's more exciting than looking down a cliff.

— GEORGE FOREMAN,
 former Olympic gold medalist and world heavyweight
 champion,
 as quoted in *Newsweek*, January 26, 1976

Once that bell rings you're on your own. It's just you and the other guy.

— JOE LOUIS,
 world heavyweight boxing champion,
 as quoted in *A Hard Road to Glory*, Arthur R. Ashe Jr.,
 1993

Bravery

Bravery is believing in yourself; that, nobody can teach you.

— EL CORDOBES,
 Spanish matador,
 as quoted in *Newsweek*, March 22, 1971

Business

There is no such money in baseball. (Babe) Ruth is the first ballplayer to get $80,000, and he will be the last. The trouble with being a club owner is that even if you are a sound businessman in your non-baseball enterprise—in my case, beer brewing and real estate—you become a fan once you get into baseball. You start doing all sorts of foolish things financially. For me, Ruth's $80,000 contract is one of those foolish things.

— COLONEL JACOB RUPPERT,
 owner of the New York Yankees from 1915 until 1939;
 quote was brought to public attention when Mickey Mantle
  and Willie Mays each signed $100,000 contracts in 1963,
  and was quoted in *The Sporting News* on March 16, 1963

Baseball, like some other sports, poses as a sacred institution dedicated to the public good, but it is actually a big, selfish business with a ruthlessness that many big businesses would never think of displaying.

— JACKIE ROBINSON,
 who broke the color barrier in 1947 as the first African-American to play major league baseball,
  in *I Never Had It Made: An Autobiography* by Jackie Robinson,
  as told to Alfred Duckett, 1972

I believe salaries are at their peak, not just in baseball, but in all sports. It's quite possible some owners will trade away, or even drop entirely, players who expect $200,000 salaries. There's a superstar born every year . . . But still there is no way clubs can continue to increase salaries to the level some players are talking about.

➤ WALTER F. O'MALLEY,
  as president of the Los Angeles Dodgers in 1971,
  as quoted in *Baseball's Greatest Quotations* by Paul Dickson,
  1991

I think $200,000 for one year is the limit any star can hope to make. I also think that the player who seeks and gets that much may be pricing himself right out of the game.

➤ WES PARKER,
  first baseman for the Los Angeles Dodgers,
  as quoted in the *Los Angeles Times,* March 24, 1971

The first principal of contract negotiation is don't remind them of what you did in the past; tell them what you're going to do in the future.

➤ STAN MUSIAL,
  Hall of Fame outfielder and senior vice president of the
    St. Louis Cardinals,
  widely attributed

I have a darn good job, but please don't ask me what I do.

➤ STAN MUSIAL,
  Hall of Fame outfielder,
  referring to his position as senior vice president of the
    St. Louis Cardinals,
  as quoted in *Sports Illustrated,* June 20, 1988

 *Careers*

If I had my life to live over again, I would do exactly as I have done. I would welcome an opportunity to play big league baseball. The old game has bestowed upon me a far wider reputation than I would ever have gained by holding test tubes over Bunsen burners in a chemical laboratory.

➤ EPPA RIXEY,
   Hall of Fame pitcher,
   referring to his early goal of being a chemist,
   as quoted in *Cooperstown Corner* by Lee Allen, 1994

What I am, what I have, what I am going to leave behind me—all this I owe to the game of baseball, without which I would have come out of the St. Mary's Industrial School in Baltimore a tailor, and a pretty bad one, at that.

➤ BABE RUTH,
   legendary Hall of Fame outfielder,
   quoted in *The Sporting News* at the time of his death on
      August 16, 1948

I started out to be a dentist. The dean of my school said, "Why don't you be an orthodontist?" That way I could have got a lot of rich kids and put a black filling in their mouth. The dean said, "Always try to be a little different." And today I make speeches all over. People ask me, "Casey, how can you speak so much when you don't talk English too good?" Well, I've been invited to Europe, and I say, "They don't speak English over there too good, either."

➤ CASEY STENGEL,
   former baseball player and manager of the New York Yankees
      and New York Mets,
   addressing an audience in 1975, a year before he died at age 85,
   as quoted after his death in the *New York Times*, April 15,
      1981

Sportswriting is the most pleasant way of making a living that man has yet devised.

⬅ RED SMITH,
  legendary sportswriter,
  widely quoted

 *Character*

My initial response was to sue her for defamation of character, but then I realized that I had no character.

⬅ CHARLES BARKLEY,
  named one of the 50 greatest players in NBA history,
  on hearing figure skater Tonya Harding proclaim herself "the
    Charles Barkley of figure skating"

The only thing that endures is character. Fame and wealth—all that is illusion. All that endures is character.

⬅ O.J. SIMPSON,
  Heisman Trophy winner and Hall of Fame football player,
    who in 1995 was accused of killing his wife, Nicole Brown
    Simpson, and her friend, Ron Goldman,
  as quoted in *The Guardian* (London), December 30, 1995,
    following his acquittal on murder charges

I can teach a lot more character winning than I can losing.

⬅ ALONZO "JAKE" GAITHER,
  former longtime football coach at Florida A&M University.
  Quote was used in Gaither's obituary in *The New York Times*,
    February 10, 1994

I want to be remembered as a Hall of Fame outfielder.

⬅ ROBERTO CLEMENTE
  who was killed in a plane crash in 1973 while on his way to
    help earthquake victims in Nicaragua;
  this quote became Clemente's epitaph

Challenge

Everest is a symbol of excellence, of the barely attainable. It is the mightiest challenge: a brutal struggle with rock, ice, altitude and self. The satisfaction comes from enduring the struggle, from doing more than you thought you could do, from rising—however briefly—above your everyday world, and from coming, momentarily, closer to the stars.

> —SUE COBB,
> U.S. athlete and mountain climber,
> from her book *The Edge of Everest*, 1989

When life gets tangled there's something so reassuring about climbing a mountain. The challenge is unambiguous.

> —STACY ALLISON,
> U.S. mountain climber, businesswoman,
> from her book, *Beyond the Limits, A Woman's Triumph on Everest*, 1999

Cheating

I didn't begin cheating until later in my career, when I needed something to help me survive. I didn't cheat when I won the 25 games in 1961. I don't want anybody to get any ideas and take my Cy Young Award away. And I didn't cheat in 1963 when I won 24 games. Well, maybe just a little.

> —WHITEY FORD,
> New York Yankees Hall of Fame pitcher,
> as quoted in his book *Slick: My Life in and Around Baseball*,
> with Phil Pepe, 1987

Ballplayers will cheat under any circumstances if they think they can get away with it. That's why we're out there. Our job is to prevent it. Only the best guys can cheat. Bang, bang, they're gone. Those slow clods can't cheat. You can spot them dashing for the base from the stands.

━NESTOR CHYLAK,
   former American League,
   as quoted in *Sport,* January 1965

Golf is like solitaire. When you cheat, you only cheat yourself.

━TONY LEMA,
   professional golfer, who was killed in a plane crash in 1966,
   as quoted in *The Golfer's Book of Wisdom*, edited by Criswell
      Freeman, 1995

No. We don't cheat. And even if we did, I'd never tell you. It's not that I don't trust you—it's all your readers I don't trust.

━TOMMY LASORDA,
   former longtime manager of the Los Angeles Dodgers,
      to a reporter in 1988,
   used by *Parade* magazine as the best baseball quote of the
      year, January 1, 1989

Cheerleaders

Getting the right players is hard. Finding cheerleaders who can count on time shouldn't be.

━MICHAEL JORDAN,
   former NBA superstar with the Chicago Bulls and director of
      basketball operations for the Washington Wizards,
   referring to the notoriously bad performances by the team's
      cheerleaders

The cheerleaders don't like us. They thought we were doing this to get dates.

➤ IMELDA CHAPARRO,
　　lineman, one of four girls who played the 1999 season on the
　　　Lincoln High School (Los Angeles) varsity football team,
　　as quoted in *Time*, November 15, 1999

Clothing

We always wore the best uniforms that money could get, Spalding saw to that. We had big wide trousers, tight-fitting jerseys, with the arms cut out clear to the shoulder, and every man had on a different cap. We wore silk stockings. When we marched on a field with our big six-footers out in front, it used to be a case of "eat 'em up, Jake." We had most of 'em whipped before we threw a ball. They were scared to death.

➤ KING KELLY,
　　nineteenth-century baseball player,
　　referring to the Chicago White Stockings of 1882,
　　as quoted in the *New York Sun*

These are my new shoes. They're good shoes. They won't make you rich like me, they won't make you rebound like me, they definitely won't make you handsome like me. They'll only make you have shoes like me. That's it.

➤ CHARLES BARKLEY,
　　named as one of the 50 greatest players in NBA history,
　　as quoted in a 1993 television commercial for basketball
　　　shoes

What difference does the uniform make? You don't hit with it.

➤ Former player and professional baseball manager,
　　on becoming coach of the Houston Astros,
　　as quoted in *The New York Times*, May 8, 1986

In addition to having proper clubs and balls, I feel that to play his best golf a golfer must feel well dressed.

—GARY PLAYER,
Hall of Fame golfer
as quoted in *Golfers on Golf*, edited by Downs MacRury, 1997

I keep a couple of phony-baloney clip-on ties in the drawer just in case, but I never dress up anymore. The worst thing I can think of is to have to put on a coat and tie every day and go to work. The last time I wore a tuxedo was in 1940. It was a rental.

—TED WILLIAMS,
legendary Hall of Fame outfielder for the Boston Red Sox,
from *My Turn at Bat: The Story of My Life*, with
John Underwood, 1988,

Knickers are good for my golf game. They're cooler in hot weather because the air circulates in them and they're warmer in cold weather because they trap the body heat.

—PAYNE STEWART,
professional golfer and two-time U.S. Open champion, who
was killed in a plane crash in October 1999,
as quoted in *Golfers on Golf*, edited by Downs MacRury,
1997

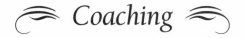

Coaching

I knew it was time to leave when they had a banquet and they gave Adolph a Cadillac and gave me a cigarette lighter.

—PAUL "BEAR" BRYANT,
legendary football coach at the University of Alabama,
as quoted when recalling his coaching days at the University
of Kentucky, where he was greatly overshadowed by
basketball coach Adolph Rupp

A rule that protects us all was broken. The decision I made was the best one for all of us. I have no choice but to stand with it. If anybody here can't live with it, go. Right now. If you stay, you do it my way, the right way, living by the rules. If you decide to stay and do it that way, we'll have a great football team. I'm going to walk out of here right now. A minute later I'm coming back in. Whoever's here, that's who we're going to play with.

   ➤ JOE PATERNO,
      longtime Penn State football head coach,
      to his players after they protested that Paterno was too strict
         when he threw one player off the team and suspended
         another for drinking beer in an airport bar following a game,
      from his book *Paterno: By the Book,* with Bernard Asbell, 1989

My greatest nightmare is thinking about what I would have missed if I had attended another school with another coach. It's not a pleasant thought. And without being overly dramatic, it is rare that a day passes that I don't think about Coach Smith in some small way for something he taught me. How do you repay someone for this type of gift?

   ➤ STEVE PREVIS,
      former student and basketball player at the University of
         North Carolina,
      referring to Dean Smith, the all-time winningest coach in
         NCAA history,
      as quoted in *The Dean's List* by Art Chansky, 1996

At Penn State, coaches are given faculty rank and they are considered to be educators. I am a full professor and two of my assistant coaches are associate professors. But there are so many colleges that refuse to recognize the football coach as anything more than a man who is in charge of jocks. Yet they put him in control of a large group of young men, give him the responsibility of molding their character and all they care about is how many football games he wins or loses. This is demeaning.

   ➤ JOE PATERNO,
      longtime football coach at Penn State,
      as quoted in *Joe Paterno: Football My Way* by Mervin D.
         Hyman and Gordon S. White Jr., 1978

Howard Cosell (former sports announcer) coaches 28 NFL teams every week, so I figure I can coach one college team.

— JOE KAPP,
    former NFL quarterback,
    after being named head football coach at California without
        any previous coaching experience

This is a private enterprise. The fans are entitled to the best product I can put on the field every Sunday, week in and week out, year in and year out. How I put that product out there is my damn business.

— BILL PARCELLS,
    former head coach of the New York Jets,
    as quoted in *ESPN SportsCentury*, edited by Michael
        MacCambridge, 1999

The country is full of good coaches. What it takes to win is a bunch of interested players.

— DON CORYELL,
    former coach of the San Diego Chargers,
    as quoted in *Get Lost Adventure Magazine*

A lifetime contract for a coach means if you're ahead in the third quarter and moving the ball, they can't fire you.

— LOU HOLTZ,
    former University of Arkansas football coach,
    as quoted in *The New York Times*, December 17, 1978

Certainly we should have a lot of coaches who are black. However, don't tell me as a Polish coach that I can't coach a kid from the inner city. I can coach anybody.

— MIKE KRZYZEWSKI,
    Duke basketball coach,
    as quoted in *ESPN SportsCentury*, edited by Michael
        MacCambridge, 1999

Something goes wrong, I yell at them—"fix it"—whether it's their fault or not. You can only really yell at the players you trust.

— BILL PARCELLS,
    former head coach of the New York Giants,
    as quoted in New York, January 26, 1987

The minute you think you've got it made, disaster is just around the corner.

➤ JOE PATERNO,
   longtime Penn State football coach,
   as quoted in *Sportswit* by Lee Green, 1984

What can you tell me I don't know? I know the bases are loaded. I know we are leading by one run. I know I have two balls on the batter. I know I have to throw a strike. I know I have to try.

➤ DON STANHOUSE,
   pitcher for the Baltimore Orioles,
   talking to pitching coach Ray Miller on the mound,
   as quoted in *Sports Illustrated*, April 16, 1979

Coaches have to watch for what they don't want to see and listen to what they don't want to hear.

➤ JOHN MADDEN,
   former coach of the Oakland Raiders from 1969 to 1979,
      turned sportscaster,
   as quoted in *The Book of Football Wisdom,* edited by Criswell
      Freeman, 1996

Commitment

Individual commitment to a group effort—that is what makes a team work, a company work, a society work, a civilization work."

➤ VINCE LOMBARDI,
   legendary Hall of Fame coach of the Green Bay Packers and
      Washington Redskins,
   in *The Speaker's Electronic Reference Collection*, AApex Soft-
      ware, 1994

I don't want to get into anything that would only be halfway. If we're going to commit to it, then we're going to commit to it all the way.

➤ AL UNSER JR.,
   Indy car driver,
   in an ESPN interview by John Kernan on *RPM2Night*

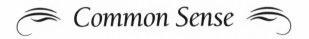

Common Sense

It's hard not to play golf that's up to Jack Nicklaus standards when you *are* Jack Nicklaus.

　—JACK NICKLAUS,
　　Hall of Fame golfer and winner of 20 major championships,
　　on winning his seventieth Professional Golf Association
　　　tournament

You've got to know when to turn around.

　—JOHN ROSKELLEY,
　　mountain climber,
　　as quoted in *The New York Times*, May 20, 1986

I just pick it up and throw it. He hit it. They scored. We didn't. That's it. It's over. It's history. Okay?

　—VIDA BLUE,
　　former major league pitcher,
　　explaining a game to a reporter,
　　from Vida: His Own Story by Bill Libby and Vida Blue, 1972

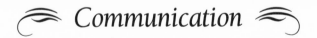

Communication

I don't communicate with players. I tell them what to do. I don't understand the meaning of communication.

　—PAUL RICHARDS,
　　former general manager of the Chicago White Sox,
　　when questioned about whether he planned to communicate
　　　with one of his players,
　　as quoted in the *New York Daily News*, January 20, 1980

Competition

Besides winning (the most fun thing is) getting out there and mixing it up with friends; it's the competition.
— AL UNSER, JR.,
   Indy car driver, two-time Indianapolis 500 winner,
   in an ESPN interview by John Kernan on *RPM2Night*

American society seems to require a No.1 or nothing at all. That is not only an unrealistic mindset, but a fairly unintelligent one.
— DEAN SMITH,
   former University of North Carolina basketball coach,
    in his book, *A Coach's Life*, 1999

The game has such a hold on golfers because they compete not only against an opponent, but also against the course, against par, and most surely—against themselves.
— GARY PLAYER,
   Hall of Fame golfer,
   as quoted in *Golfers on Golf*, edited by Downs MacRury, 1997

Concentration

You can win tournaments when you're mechanical, but golf is a game of emotion and adjustment. If you're not aware of what's happening to your mind and your body when you're playing, you'll never be able to be the very best you can be.
— JACK NICKLAUS,
   Hall of Fame golfer and winner of 20 major championships,
   as quoted in *Golfers on Golf*, edited by Downs MacRury, 1997

Concentration is the most fragile thing I know. A team that loses concentration can't win. A coach that loses concentration cannot lead a team to win. A coach and team that take winning for granted—or dwell on losses—lose concentration. A winning team and coach have to run scared without letup—but also without actually getting scared. Getting scared destroys concentration.

➤JOE PATERNO,
longtime Penn State football coach,
from his book, *Paterno: By the Book*, with Bernard Asbell, 1989

Golf takes more mental energy, more concentration, more determination than any other sport ever invented.

➤ARNOLD PALMER, Hall of Fame golfer, as quoted in *Golfers on Golf*, edited by Downs MacRury, 1997

I just try to concentrate on concentrating.

➤MARTINA NAVRATILOVA,
Hall of Fame tennis player,
as quoted in *US* magazine, October 20, 1986

It is necessary to relax your muscles when you can. Relaxing your brain is fatal.

➤STIRLING MOSS,
English racing driver, who retired in 1962 after a serious accident,
as quoted in *Newsweek*, May 16, 1955

Concentration is the ability to think about absolutely nothing when it is absolutely necessary.

➤RAY KNIGHT ,
former major league player and manager, turned broadcaster,
as quoted in *Get Lost Adventure Magazine*

When I'm in this state, everything is pure, vividly clear. I'm in a cocoon of concentration.

➤TONY JACKLIN,
former professional golfer,
as quoted in *Golfers on Golf*, edited by Downs MacRury, 1997

When I'm in a zone, I don't think about the shot or the wind or the distance or the gallery or anything; I just pull a club and swing.

—MARK CALCAVECCHIA,
professional golfer,
as quoted in *Golfers on Golf*, edited by Downs MacRury, 1997

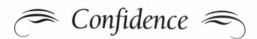

Confidence

Once you have the confidence, once your swing and everything has given your mind confidence, then it is all mental. Your mind will automatically tell you, "Do this. Do that."

—NICK FALDO,
Hall of Fame golfer,
as quoted in *Golfers On Golf*, edited by Downs MacRury, 1997

For many of us who struggle with "fitting in" or our identity—sports gives us our first face of confidence. That first bit of confidence can be a gateway to many other great things!

—DAN O'BRIEN,
world-class decathlon athlete, who was adopted at age 2,
as quoted in *The Most Important Thing I Know about the Spirit of Sport*, compiled by Lorne A. Adrain, 1999

You'll never increase your driving distance without a positive mental attitude. Confidence is vital.

—GREG NORMAN,
Australian golfer, also known as the "Great White Shark,"
as quoted in *Golfers On Golf*, edited by Downs MacRury, 1997

Confidence, without ability, is impossible to maintain. You can't feel confident very long if you don't know how to hit the ball.

—DOUG FORD,
professional golfer,
as quoted in *Golfers On Golf*, edited by Downs MacRury, 1997

I played poorly for so long that I lost all confidence. I found out it takes a long time to overcome all negative thoughts.

> ← BOB TWAY,
>> professional golfer and winner of the 1986 PGA
>> Championship,
>> as quoted in *Golfers On Golf*, edited by Downs MacRury, 1997

Confidence is everything. From there, it's a small step to winning.

> ← CRAIG STADLER,
>> professional golfer,
>> as quoted in *Golfers On Golf*, edited by Downs MacRury, 1997

Certainly, when I teach people windsurfing, one of the things I really work on is building up their confidence and enthusiasm in themselves. It is surprising the number of people who don't have that, who go through life fearful all the time.

> ← EDWARD BISHOP,
>> who at 71 years old was windsurfing and teaching others in
>> the San Francisco area to windsurf,
>> as quoted in *December Champions* by Bob Darden and W.R.
>> Spence, M.D., 1993

You've got to take the initiative and play your game. In a decisive set, confidence is the difference.

> ← CHRIS EVERT,
>> Hall of Fame tennis player,
>> as quoted in *The Ultimate Success Quotations Library*, Cyber
>> Nation International, Inc., Reno, NV, 1997

During my winning streaks I got to the point where I thought I was never going to lose. Everything was so automatic and so easy. I was so confident, I felt no one could beat me.

> ← NANCY LOPEZ,
>> Hall of Fame golfer,
>> as quoted in *Golfers On Golf*, edited by Downs MacRury, 1997

Consequences

I'm my own man. I make my own decisions. If they're right or wrong, I have to live with them.

—SCOTTIE PIPPEN,
    named one of the 50 greatest players in NBA history,
    as quoted in *Sports Illustrated*, December 13, 1999

Controversy

We have almost no controversy. Maybe I should get in a fistfight with Jack Nicklaus on the eighteenth green.

—TOM WATSON,
    Hall of Fame golfer,
    referring to golf's modest television ratings,
    as quoted in *Golfers On Golf*, edited by Downs MacRury, 1997

Courage

You discover within yourself a greater courage, a greater perspective than you ever knew you had.

—ROLF BENIRSCHKE,
    former San Diego Chargers placekicker,
    after his third surgery for ulcerative colitis

Where is the university for courage? . . . The university for courage is to do what you believe in!

— EL CORDOBES,
   Spanish matador,
   in *Or I'll Dress You in Mourning*, New American Library, 1970

Bravery is teaching yourself, and that thing nobody can teach you.

— EL CORDOBES,
   Spanish matador,
   as quoted in *Newsweek*, March 22, 1971

Cultural Differences

New Yorkers love it when you spill your guts out there. Spill your guts at Wimbledon and they make you stop and clean it up.

— JIMMY CONNORS,
   Hall of Fame tennis player,
   as quoted in *Guardian*, "Sports Quotes of the Year," December 24, 1984

A player's got to be kept hungry to become a big leaguer. That's why no boy from a rich family ever made the big leagues.

— JOE DiMAGGIO,
   former New York Yankees outfielder and Hall of Fame member,
   as quoted in the *New York Times*, April 30, 1961

Kansas City fans don't know how to be mean. They know how to be mean in Philadelphia.

— LARRY BOWA,
   former Philadelphia Phillies shortstop,
   during the Philadelphia-Kansas City World Series, 1980

The biggest thing I don't like about New York are the foreigners. I'm not a very big fan of foreigners. You can walk an entire block in Times Square and not hear anybody speaking English. Asians and Koreans and Vietnamese and Indians and Russians and Spanish people and everything up there. How the hell did they get in this country?

> —JOHN ROCKER,
> relief pitcher for the Atlanta Braves,
> discussing his dislike for New York City,
> in *Sports Illustrated*, November, 1999.
> He was suspended and fined for his remarks.

One more thing, when Russians talk to you, or at least to me, they get really close to you. With some people you feel as if you are about to die because they have bad breath.

> —VENUS WILLIAMS,
> professional tennis player,
> from an online diary she kept for the Women's Tennis
> Association website during her trip to Russia in October
> 1997 to play in the Ladies Kremlin Cup

 *Danger*

Motor racing is dangerous, but what is danger? It is dangerous to climb a mountain. It is dangerous to cross main roads. It is dangerous to explore a jungle. One cannot frame regulations to make everything safe.

> —MIKE HAWTHORN,
> English racing driver, who, driving for Ferrari, won the For-
> mula One World Championship in 1958, retired from the
> sport, and was killed in a road accident in 1959,
> as quoted in *The Guinness Dictionary of Sports Quotations*
> by Colin Jarman, 1990.

If everyone were like him, I wouldn't play. I'd find a safer way to make a living.

— ANDY VAN SLYKE,
  former major league baseball player,
  after relief pitcher Mitch "Wild Thing" Williams nearly hit
      him twice in the head while striking him out,
  as quoted in *The Sporting News,* July 17, 1989

Death

Well, we're all 10 years older today. Dizzy Dean is dead. And 1934 is gone forever. Another part of our youth's fled. You look in the mirror and the small boy no longer smiles back at you. Just that sad old man. The Gashouse Gang is now a duet. Dizzy died the other day at the age of 11 or 12. The little boy in all of us died with him . . .

— JIM MURRAY,
  legendary sportswriter and Pulitzer Prize winner,
  on the death of baseball player Dizzy Dean,
  as it appeared in the *Los Angeles Times,* July 19, 1974

The Big Guy's left us with the night to face, and there is no one who can take his place.

— GRANTLAND RICE,
  legendary sportswriter,
  writing about the death of Babe Ruth

We used to tease each other about whose liver was going to go first. I never thought it would end for him this way.

— MICKEY MANTLE,
  legendary New York Yankees outfielder and Hall of Famer,
  referring to the death of his Yankees teammate, Billy Martin,
  as quoted in *USA Today,* December 29, 1989

It's great to be out here again. I tell you, if I'm going to blow out someday, I want it to be at the ballpark. Really, it'd be great. I'd blow out, they'd cart me around the field a couple of times, the fans would cheer, and then, poof, out the main gate. Gone.

➤ BOB UECKER,
    former major league catcher, who later became a broadcaster,
    returning to the broadcast booth following a mild heart attack
        at age 54,
    as quoted in the *Washington Times*, March 6, 1989

Well, that kind of puts a damper on even a Yankee win.

➤ PHIL RIZZUTO,
    former New York Yankees shortstop, turned Yankees
        broadcaster sportscaster,
    reacting to a news bulletin that Pope Paul VI had died on
        August 6, 1978

I was closer to (Ray) Chapman than anyone else on earth, and right now, almost 30 years later, I still believe it was an accident, pure and simple. You know, Chapman had a peculiar stance. It is literally true that he could have been hit on the head by a perfect strike. He crowded the plate and hunched over it. His head was in the strike zone. That's what happened the day he was killed. I saw the pitch coming. I saw Ray standing there never moving so much as a muscle. He must have been paralyzed, fascinated like the rabbit by the snake. Then I heard the crack. I can hear it yet. It sounded exactly like a fastball meeting the bat. I saw the ball roll toward the pitcher's box. I was just a kid then, and pretty fast on my feet. I pounced across the plate, snatched up the ball and fired it toward first base. Only then did I see the look on Carl Mays' face. I turned around, Chappie was half-sitting, half-sprawling in the batter's box. I tried to rush to him, but [Tris] Speaker and Steve O'Neill and Jack Graney got there ahead of me. I guess I was glued to the ground. I knew right then that I had seen a man killed by a baseball.

➤ MUDDY RUEL,
    New York Yankees catcher,
    referring to the death of Ray Chapman when Chapman was
        struck by a Carl Mays pitch during the 1920 season,
    as quoted in *The Sporting News* in 1948

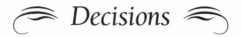

Decisions

Today the biggest decisions I make aren't related to the heavy-weight title. They are whether I visit McDonalds, Burger King, Wendy's or Jack-in-the-Box.

—GEORGE FOREMAN,
    Olympic gold medalist and former world heavyweight
        champion,
    from *The Speaker's Electronic Reference Collection*, AApex
        Software, 1994

Diet

I don't actually have a strict diet regimen, but I eat simply. I mostly eat carbohydrates, fresh vegetables—I grow my own in season—and fresh fruits. I do have a weakness that sets in in the colder weather, however. I will sometimes give in to chocolate candies, chocolate chip cookies, and ice cream—although I've switched to frozen yogurt. I will eat meat if I am out with friends, but I only cook it sparingly myself, maybe twice a week. I just try to keep a well-rounded diet, but I do believe in vitamin supplements.

—SISTER MADONNA BUTLER,
    a Spokane, Washington, Catholic nun, who at age 62 was
        setting records in Ironman triathlon events,
    as quoted in *December Champions* by Bob Darden and W.R.
        Spence, M.D., 1993

Scallions are the greatest cure for a batting slump.

—BABE RUTH,
    Hall of Fame outfielder,
    referring to his practice of eating his way out of a slump,
    as quoted in *Baseball's Greatest Quotations* by Paul Dickson,
        1991

I haven't had a mouthful of meat, fish or fowl since before I was 18. The animals get their food from vegetarian sources and when we eat meat, we get it second-hand! And so we vegetarians have learned to make many interesting dishes that are the main dish, the protein dish. We eat all kinds of different things. Of course, you don't need to. You could eat very simply. I use milk. Maybe a cup a day. There are protein dishes from beans, peas and greens. If you're not a vegetarian, you'd be surprised what tasty dishes vegetarians make out of the plant foods.

➤ HULDA CROOKS,
   a Loma Linda, California, grandmother, who at age 91
      climbed the 14,494-foot Mount Whitney for the twenty-
      third time,
   as quoted in *December Champions* by Bob Darden and W.R.
      Spence, M.D., 1993

Desire

What does it take to be a champion? Desire, dedication, determination, concentration and the will to win.

➤ PATTY BERT,
   Hall of Fame golfer and a founder of the Ladies Professional
      Golf Association tour,
   as quoted in *Golfers on Golf*, edited by Downs MacRury,
      1997

Desire is the bottom line. You've got to have 100 percent desire. Anything less is complacency.

➤ TOM WATSON,
   Hall of Fame golfer,
   as quoted in *Golfers on Golf*, edited by Downs MacRury,
      1997

 *Disgust*

I've had a belly full. When I look at some of those construction workers in New York, climbing around 20 stories high, working for their bucks the way they do, and a cab driver eight or 10 hours a day . . . and I see how hard these guys work, and then they come out here (to the ballpark) and they pay their good money to see what happened last night, when we (the Yankees) got wiped out 14-2, in a lackadaisical performance, that gets to me. I'm tired of complaining. Baseball players should be the happiest guys in the world. They're being paid megabucks for playing a kid's game.

— GEORGE STEINBRENNER,
    controversial owner of the New York Yankees,
    as quoted on the *CBS Morning News*, August 5, 1982

They aren't even worth watching!

— GEORGE STEINBRENNER,
    controversial owner of the New York Yankees,
    referring to his team, which played so badly in a double-
        header against the White Sox on August 3, 1982, that
        Steinbrenner told all the fans at the game that they could
        come to another game without paying

 *Diversity*

It's really nice seeing more minorities in the gallery. I think that's where the game (golf) should go and will go.

— TIGER WOODS,
    professional golfer,
    as quoted in *Golfers on Golf*, edited by Downs MacRury, 1997

Seven out of 10 black faces you see on television are athletes. The black athlete carries the image of the black community. He carries the cross, in a way, until blacks make inroads in other dimensions.

➤ ARTHUR ASHE,
   Hall of Fame tennis player and AIDS activist
   in *The New York Public Library Book of 20th Century American Quotations* by Stephen Donadio, 1992

Growing up, I came up with this name: I'm a Cablinasian.

➤ TIGER WOODS,
   professional golfer,
   explaining during an interview with Oprah Winfrey on April 21, 1997, why he doesn't think that African-American accurately describes his ancestry of Caucasian, Afro-American, Native American, Chinese, and Thai

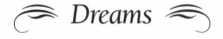

Dreams

What I've learned in my years as a competitive wheelchair athlete is this—what separates a winner from the rest of the pack is not raw talent or physical ability; instead it is the drive and dedication to work hard every single day, and the heart to go after your dream, no matter how unattainable others think it is.

➤ LINDA MASTANDREA,
   world champion athlete, lawyer, and community leader, who has been in a wheelchair for 15 years due to cerebral palsy,
   as quoted in *The Most Important Thing I Know about the Spirit of Sport*, compiled by Lorne A. Adrain, 1999

Any skater dreams of being the world champion. It would be a dream come true.

➤ MICHELLE KWAN,
   champion figure skater,
   as quoted in *Born to Skate: The Michelle Kwan Story* by Edward Z. Epstein, 1997

The last time I put on this uniform, I think I was 8— for a father-son game. This is something I dreamed about as a little kid, being back in my hometown where I watched so many great players.

➤ KEN GRIFFEY JR.,
major league baseball player,
announcing that he'll return home to play for the Cincinnati Reds, even though he'll make less money than if he'd have stayed with the Seattle Mariners or become a free agent,
as quoted in *Newsweek*, February 21, 2000

Ever since I retired, I keep having these dreams. The worst one is I go to the ballpark late, jump out of a cab, and I hear 'em calling my name on the public address system. I try and get in and all the gates are locked. Then I see a hole under the fence and I can see Casey (Stengel) looking for me, and Yogi (Berra) and Billy Martin and Whitey Ford. I try to crawl through the hole and I get stuck at the hips. And that's where I wake up, sweating.

➤ MICKEY MANTLE,
New York Yankees outfielder and Hall of Famer, ,
as quoted in *High Inside: Memoirs of a Baseball Wife* by Danielle Gagnon Torrez, 1993

There's sort of a universal wish among us all to be the great American sports hero. Thurber once said that 95 percent of the male population puts themselves to sleep striking out the lineup of the New York Yankees. It's the great daydream, an idea that you never quite give up. Always, somewhere in the back of your mind, you believe Casey Stengel will give you a call.

➤ GEORGE PLIMPTON,
noted author,
as quoted in the *Dallas Times-Herald's* "Sportsweek," December 15, 1978

Drugs

A cloud hangs over baseball. It's a cloud called drugs and it's permeated our game.

— PETER UEBERROTH,
former major league baseball commissioner,
as quoted in the *New York Times*, September 25, 1985

There are enough players on a team that will take a bat in their hand and take you into a room if they think you're using drugs. There's enormous peer pressure.

— PETER UEBERROTH,
former major league baseball commissioner,
as quoted in *USA Today*, February 19, 1988

When I came over here, I always heard it was a stronger league, with amphetamines all over the clubhouse, but all I found was Michelob Dry.

— DAN QUISENBERRY,
former relief pitcher,
referring to his move from the American League's Kansas City
Royals to the National League's St. Louis Cardinals,
as quoted in *The Sporting News*, April 3, 1989

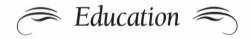

Education

I wish there was some way I could have gotten a college education. I'm thinking about buying a college, though.

— PETE ROSE,
former major league baseball player and the all-time hits
leader,
as quoted in *Sports Illustrated*, May 2, 1988

Ego

Egotism is the anesthetic that dulls the pain of stupidity.

➤ FRANK LEAHY,
    legendary college football coach whose record of 87-11-9 at
       Notre Dame was second only to that of Knute Rockne,
    as quoted in *Look* magazine, January 10, 1955

Isn't that something? The egos are such that they can accept the accolades, but they'd beat you over the head for writing what they did wrong. And all you're looking at is the facts.

➤ DALLAS GREEN,
    former major league pitcher, manager, and front office execu-
       tive,
    referring to players hiding in the trainer's room to avoid
       reporters,
    as quoted in *The Sporting News*, May 8, 1989

A long drive is good for the ego.

➤ ARNOLD PALMER,
    Hall of Fame golfer,
    as quoted in *Golfers on Golf*, edited by Downs MacRury, 1997

Baseball is a tremendous business for men with big egos. But ego can only take you so far. After that, it has to be a good business proposition.

➤ BRAD CORBETT,
    former owner of the Texas Rangers,
    explaining why he sold the team

There are two things no man will admit he can't do well—drive and make love.

➤ STIRLING MOSS,
    English racing driver, who retired in 1962 after a serious
       crash,
    as quoted in *The Guinness Dictionary of Sports Quotations*
       by Colin Jarman, 1990

For some people, life outside the spotlight is death.

➤NADIA COMANECI,
    former Rumanian gymnast,
    in *The Astonishing World* by Barbara Grizzuti Harrison,
        1992

The more self-centered and egotistical a guy is, the better ballplayer he's going to be. You take a team with 25 assholes and I'll show you a pennant. I'll show you the New York Yankees.

➤BILL LEE,
    professional baseball pitcher,
    from *Baseball's Greatest Quotations*, by Paul Dickson, 1991

I like the moment when I break a man's ego.

➤BOBBY FISCHER,
    former world champion chess player,
    as quoted in *Newsweek*, July 31, 1972

 *Encouragement*

I always wanted to be somebody . . . If I've made it, it's half because I was game to take a wicked amount of punishment along the way and half because there were an awful lot of people who cared enough to help me.

➤ALTHEA GIBSON,
    Hall of Fame tennis player and the first African-American
        player to win the U.S. Open and Wimbledon
        championships,
    from her book *I Always Wanted to Be Somebody*, 1958

Enthusiasm

If you aren't fired with enthusiasm, you'll be fired with enthusiasm.

—VINCE LOMBARDI,
    legendary coach of the Green Bay Packers and Washington
        Redskins,
    when talking to his team,
    as quoted in *Sportswit* by Lee Green, 1984

Equal Rights

As a matter of fact I do not deserve any recognition from anybody on the (Jackie) Robinson thing. It is a terrible commentary on all of us that a part of us should not concede equal right to everybody to earn a living.

—BRANCH RICKEY,
    major league baseball innovator and president-general man-
        ager of the Brooklyn Dodgers, who integrated professional
        baseball in 1947 by bringing up Jackie Robinson,
    as quoted in *Branch Rickey* by Murray Polner

I believe that racial extractions and color hues and forms of worship become secondary to what men can do. The American public is not as concerned with a first baseman's pigmentation as it is with the power of his swing, the dexterity of his slide, and the gracefulness of his fielding or the speed of his legs.

—BRANCH RICKEY,
    major league baseball innovator and president-general man-
        ager of the Brooklyn Dodgers, who integrated professional
        baseball in 1947 by bringing up Jackie Robinson,
    as quoted in *Reader's Digest*, February 1949

Black players have saved baseball, kept baseball on top. But I think football and basketball have moved beyond baseball in race relations; in many instances, they hire a man to do a job regardless of his skin color. Baseball is still wallowing around in the 19th century, saying a black can't manage, a black can't go into the front office . . . I think baseball is very vindictive. I think, very frankly, that a black man who is willing to accept their dictates and do what they want him to do can get along beautifully. But if you're a man and you stand on your own two feet, then look out. I think this is basically the problem today with baseball.

➤JACKIE ROBINSON,
> former Brooklyn Dodgers infielder and the first black player
> to play in the major leagues,
> as quoted in the *New York Times*, December 5, 1971

Excuses

Honey, I just forgot to duck.

➤JACK DEMPSEY,
> legendary world heavyweight champion,
> to his wife after losing the world heavyweight title on Sept.
> 23, 1926

I zigged when I should have zagged.

➤Boxer JACK ROPER,
> explaining how he was knocked out by heavyweight
> champion Joe Louis on April 17, 1939

I had such a good year I didn't want to forget it.

➤DICK STUART,
> former first baseman for the Boston Red Sox,
> explaining to a policeman why he still had 1963 plates on his
> car in 1964

I wasn't in a slump. I just wasn't getting any hits.

⬤—DAVE HENDERSON,
former major league baseball player after ending an
0-for-20 slump,
as quoted in *USA Today*, April 23, 1990

There are a thousand reasons for failure, but not a single excuse.

⬤—MIKE REID,
former Cincinnati Bengals All-Pro defensive lineman,
quoted in *Sportswit* by Lee Green, 1984

Expectations

I don't see anyone playing in the major leagues today who combines both the talent and the intensity that I had. I always tried to do the best; I knew I couldn't always be the best, but I tried to be. I expect that of my players today and of my kids. My wife says I shouldn't expect that of my children but I don't think that's asking too much.

⬤—FRANK ROBINSON,
two-time winner of the Triple Crown and major league baseball's first black manager,
on his election to the Baseball Hall of Fame on January 14, 1982

As you think, so shall you become.

⬤—BRUCE LEE,
U.S. martial arts expert,
from *The Ultimate Success Quotations Library*, Cyber Nation International, Inc., Reno, NV, 1997

I like to expect the unexpected.

⬤—GREG NORMAN,
Australian golfer, also known as the "Great White Shark,
as quoted in *Golfers on Golf*, edited by Downs MacRury, 1997

I'm not in this world to live up to your expectations and you're not in this world to live up to mine.

> ➤BRUCE LEE,
> martial arts expert,
> In *The Ultimate Success Quotations Library*, Cyber Nation
> International, Inc., Reno, NV, 1997

One of the things that my parents have taught me is never listen to other people's expectations. You should live your own life and live up to your own expectations, and those are the only things I really care about it.

> ➤TIGER WOODS,
> professional golfer,
> in "An Interview with Tiger Woods" on www.golf.com

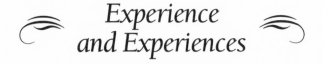

Experience and Experiences

Perhaps the single most important element in mastering the techniques and tactics of racing is experience. But once you have the fundamentals, acquiring the experience is a matter of time.

> ➤GREG LEMOND,
> former world-class cyclist and winner of the Tour de France,
> as quoted in *Get Lost Adventure Magazine*

Experience is a great advantage. The problem is that when you get the experience, you're too damned old to do anything about it.

> ➤JIMMY CONNORS,
> Hall of Fame tennis player,
> in the *Ultimate Success Quotations Library*, Cyber Nation
> International, Inc., Reno, NV, 1997

Experience is a hard teacher because she gives the test first, the lesson afterward.

—VERNON LAW,
former pitcher for the Pittsburgh Pirates,
as quoted in *This Week*, August 14, 1960

The young player has strength and energy, but envies the experiences of the older player.

—GARY PLAYER,
Hall of Fame golfer,
as quoted in *Golfers on Golf*, edited by Downs MacRury, 1997

Through years of experience I have found that air offers less resistance than dirt.

—JACK NICKLAUS,
Hall of Fame golfer and winner of 20 major championships,
as quoted in *Golfers on Golf*, edited by Downs MacRury, 1997

I like to collect experiences the way other people like to collect coins and stamps.

—MICHAEL MCGUIRE,
adventurer,
on hiking across the polar ice cap,
as quoted in the *Christian Science Monitor*, February 26, 1985

Well, so much for not having any experience in the playoffs.

—St. Louis Rams coach DICK VERMEIL,
after his team beat the Minnesota Vikings 49-37 in the
National Football Conference divisional playoff game in
January 2000

The Extra Mile

It's not enough just to swing at the ball. You've got to loosen your girdle and let 'er fly.

— BABE DIDRIKSON ZAHARIAS,
   Hall of Fame golfer, sportswoman, and Olympic champion,
   relating her formula for female success in *WomenSports*
      magazine, November 1975

Failure

I've missed more than 9,000 shots. I've lost almost 300 games. Twenty-six times, I've been trusted to take the game-winning shot, and missed.

— MICHAEL JORDAN,
   former NBA superstar with the Chicago Bulls,
   in a Nike ad that aired in 1997, showing him missing shots
      and losing games

I have always felt that although someone may defeat me, and I strike out in a ballgame, the pitcher on that particular day was the best player. But I know when I see him again, I'm going to be ready for his curve ball. Failure is a part of success.

— HANK AARON,
   the all-time home run leader and Hall of Famer,
   as quoted in the *Ultimate Success Quotations Library,* Cyber
      Nation International, Inc., Reno, NV, 1997

Golf is mostly a game about failures.

— TOMMY AARON,
   professional golfer,
   as quoted in *Golfers on Golf*, edited by Downs MacRury, 1997

I think I fail a bit less than everyone else.

➤ JACK NICKLAUS,
 Hall of Fame golfer and winner of 20 major championships,
 as quoted in *The Golf Quotations Book* by Michael Hobbs, 1992

I'm ready for it. I'm not afraid to fail. I'm a strong enough person to accept failure. But, I'm not going to accept not trying.

➤ MICHAEL JORDAN,
 former NBA superstar with the Chicago Bulls,
 after announcing on February 7, 1994, that he'd signed a
 minor league contract with the Chicago White Sox

Success is never final. Failure is never fatal.

➤ JOE PATERNO,
 longtime Penn State football coach,
 in *The Book of Football Wisdom*, edited by Criswell Freeman,
 1996

I was so apprehensive. I got so many over par and felt the whole of Australia had sat up all night watching me screw up. I believed I had failed. But after about a week I realized that just because you fail, it doesn't make you a failure.

➤ IAN BAKER-FINCH,
 professional golfer,
 after his fourth-round 79 in the 1984 British Open, which
 he'd led after three rounds

The traditions of the game are rich with memories of dramatic triumphs as well as heartbreaking failures. The best players fail the most because they are in the hunt all the time. You learn to handle it—accept it or you don't survive.

➤ DEANE BEMAN,
 professional golfer and former commissioner of the
 Professional Golf Association tour,
 as quoted in *Golfers on Golf*, edited by Downs MacRury,
 1997

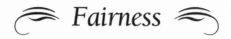

Fairness

He's fair. He treats us all the same—like dogs.

➤HENRY JORDAN,
former Green Bay Packers right tackle,
referring to Coach Vince Lombardi

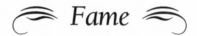

Fame

Being a celebrity is like being raped, and there's absolutely nothing
a player can do about it.

➤JOHN MCENROE,
Hall of Fame tennis player and United States Davis Cup captain,
as quoted in *The Guinness Dictionary of Sports Quotations*
by Colin Jarman, 1990.

What do you do after you are world famous and 19 or 20 and you
have sat with prime ministers, kings and queens, the Pope? Do you
go back home and take a job? What do you do to keep your sanity?
You come back to the real world.

➤WILMA RUDOLPH,
U.S. track athlete and winner of three gold medals in the
1960 Olympics,
as quoted in *I Dream a World* by Brian Lanker, 1989

Fans

I occasionally get birthday cards from fans. But it's often the same message: They hope it's my last.

➤ AL FORMAN,
former National League umpire,
as quoted in *Time*, August 25, 1961

The autograph stuff drives me crazy. People are dangerous.

➤ MICHAEL JORDAN,
former NBA superstar with the Chicago Bulls,
referring to an incident in which he was nearly stampeded in
Houston,
as quoted in *Playboy*, May 1992

We don't need that hooting and hollering.

➤ BILL CAMPBELL,
former president of the United States Golf Association,
referring to Tiger Woods' sometimes exuberant fans,
as quoted in *Sports Illustrated*, July 21, 1997

People feel that because they see you all the time they know you and can say something whether they like you or dislike you.

➤ GREG NORMAN,
professional golfer,
as quoted in *Sports Illustrated*, July 21, 1997

You're trying your damndest, you strike out and they boo you. I act like it doesn't bother me, like I don't hear anything the fans say, but the truth is I hear every word of it and it kills me.

➤ MIKE SCHMIDT,
former Hall of Fame third baseman for the Philadelphia
Phillies,
widely quoted

These fans are very rabid, like they were very collegiate or something because it takes four hours for us to leave our dressing room after a game, which is good because the concessions people sell a lot of hot dogs, which is good for our business and I like that. I expect that very soon they will carry one of my players out on their shoulders like he just caught the winning touchdown for Yale. They are very patient and that's good. These fellows of ours are going to keep right on improving because they're better than most folks think and not as bad as they used to be. Because it would be hard to be as bad as that.

—CASEY STENGEL,
    former manager of the New York Yankees and the New York
      Mets,
    describing Mets fans during the team's infancy in the early
      1960s,
    as quoted in *The Sporting News,* October 18, 1975

They read their sports pages, know their statistics and either root like hell or boo our butts off. I love it. Give me vocal fans—pro or con—over the tourist-types who show up in Houston or Montreal and just sit there.

—MIKE SCHMIDT,
    former Hall of Fame third baseman for the Philadelphia
      Phillies,
    referring to Phillies fans,
    as quoted in the *Los Angeles Times,* March 31, 1975

I know the fans will be back eventually. They can't get this kind of entertainment for the price anywhere. It's like a guy who goes to a smorgasbord and gets a big plate of food for two dollars and gets insulted. But still he goes back again because he knows he can't get that kind of food anywhere else for that kind of money.

—TOMMY LASORDA,
    former manager of the Los Angeles Dodgers
    referring to the 1981 baseball players' strike,
    as quoted in the *Washington Star,* July 31, 1981

Philly fans are so mean that one Easter Sunday, when the players staged an Easter egg hunt for their kids, the fans booed the kids who didn't find any eggs. They even boo the National Anthem.

➤ BOB UECKER,
  former Philadelphia Phillies catcher, turned broadcaster,
  as quoted in the *Los Angeles Times*, April 1, 1971

Those bums don't scare me. I'm going to win it.

➤ SAM SNEAD,
  Hall of Fame golfer, who won a record 81 PGA tournaments
    and 7 major titles,
  responding to fans who were heckling him during the final
    round of the 1942 PGA tournament in Atlantic City

But I'll tell you this—I made up my mind a long time ago not to get too excited, no matter which way the crowd goes. I get paid for playing left field and for hitting that baseball. I am not a participant in a popularity contest.

➤ TED WILLIAMS,
  legendary Hall of Fame outfielder for the Boston Red Sox,
  as quoted in the *Saturday Evening Post*, April 10, 1954

The fan is the one who suffers. He cheers a guy to a .350 season, then watches that player sign with another team. When you destroy fan loyalties, you destroy everything.

➤ FRANK ROBINSON,
  Hall of Fame outfielder and major league baseball's first black
    manager,
  referring to free agents during his tenure as coach of the
    Baltimore Orioles

They know when to cheer and they know when to boo. And they know when to drink beer. They do it all the time.

➤ GORMAN THOMAS,
  a baseball player formerly with the Milwaukee Brewers,
  referring to Brewer fans,
  as quoted in the (Baltimore) *Sun*, April 26, 1987

Those fans say things about your mother that make you want to get up in the stands and punch a few of them.

➤ JIM "MUDCAT" GRANT,
former major league pitcher,
from *Joy in Mudville* by George Vecsey, 1970

I owe everything I have to them when I'm out there on the mound. But I owe the fans nothing and they owe me nothing when I am not pitching.

➤ CHRISTY MATHEWSON,
Hall of Fame pitcher,
referring to his relationship with the fans,
as quoted in *The Tumult and the Shouting* by Grantland Rice,
1954

Hey, big mouth, how do you spell triple?

➤ "SHOELESS" JOE JACKSON,
Negro League superstar, who was illiterate,
said to a fan who'd been heckling him by repeatedly asking
him if he could spell "illiterate," after Jackson hit a triple

When they boo you, you know they mean you.

➤ GEORGE HALAS,
legendary Hall of Fame coach of the Chicago Bears,
referring to San Francisco, his "favorite booing city"

 *Fear*

What you have got to remember is that it is the panic rather than the one miscreant shot which will make the difference between a good round and bad.

➤ LAURA DAVIES,
professional golfer,
as quoted in *Golfers on Golf*, edited by Downs MacRury, 1997

I fear nobody but the dentist.

 ➤VIKTOR KORCHNOI,
  chess grand master,
  when asked if he feared playing Russian grand master Anatoly
    Karpov for the world championship in 1978

When you're my size in the pros, fear is a sign that you're not stupid.

 ➤JERRY LEVIAS,
  Houston Oilers kick returner,
  as quoted when talking about his size (5 feet, 9 inches; 177
    pounds)

I know that fear is an obstacle for some people, but it is an illusion to me . . . Failure always made me try harder next time.

 ➤MICHAEL JORDAN,
  former NBA superstar,
  as quoted in *I Can't Accept Not Trying: Michael Jordan on the
    Pursuit of Excellence*, 1994

The person I fear most in the last two rounds is myself.

 ➤TOM WATSON,
  Hall of Fame golfer,
  as quoted in *Golfers on Golf*, edited by Downs MacRury,
    1997

After 12 years the old butterflies came back. Well, I guess at my age you call them moths.

 ➤FRANCO HARRIS,
  Pittsburgh Steelers Hall of Fame running back,
  when he started playing for a new team (Seattle Seahawks),
  as quoted in *Sports Illustrated*, October 1, 1984

Pitching is . . . the art of instilling fear.

 ➤SANDY KOUFAX,
  Hall of Fame pitcher for the Los Angeles Dodgers,
  as quoted in *The Gashouse Gang* by Robert Hood, 1976

I shot a wild elephant in Africa 30 yards from me, and it didn't hit the ground until it was right at my feet. I wasn't a bit scared. But a four-foot putt scares me to death.

 ⟵SAM SNEAD,
   Hall of Fame golfer and winner of a record 81 Professional
     Golf Association tournaments,
   as quoted in *Golfers on Golf,* edited by Downs MacRury, 1997

I was nervous, so I read the New Testament. I read the verse about have no fear, and I felt relaxed. Then I jumped farther than I ever jumped before in my life.

 ⟵WILLYE WHITE,
   U.S. 1956 Olympic silver medalist,
   as quoted in *Life*, Summer 1984

Of all the hazards, fear is the worst.

 ⟵SAM SNEAD,
   Hall of Fame golfer and the winner of a record 81 Profes-
     sional Golf Association tournaments,
   as quoted in *Golfers on Golf*, edited by Downs MacRury, 1997

I've been nervous all week. Now I'm just bloody terrified.

 ⟵TONY JACKLIN,
   professional golfer,
   speaking before the final round of the 1969 British Open,
     which he won

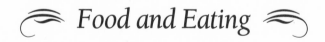

Food and Eating

Be sure to put some of them neutrons on it.

 ⟵MIKE SMITH,
   professional baseball player,
   instructing a waitress on how to prepare his salad

I was so elated that we had finally won the world championship that I spent the entire winter eating. Of course, had we lost, I would have been so unhappy I would have spent the entire winter eating.

    —TOMMY LASORDA,
        former manager of the Los Angeles Dodgers
        referring to the 1981 World Series,
        from his book *The Artful Dodger*, 1985

It was the first time a game has ever been called on account of candy bars.

    —DICK SCHAAP,
        author and commentator,
        referring to the Reggie candy bars that fans threw onto the
           field after Reggie Jackson scored a home run

Now, I do love desserts. I want you to know my wife makes great desserts. And in my cereal each morning I use half and half. I couldn't enjoy my cereal without half and half. I love soups. For a meal, maybe I'll have a glass of wine, a bowl of soup, and dessert. If I make soup at home out of a can, I use half and half. If I have one bad habit, it is maybe desserts. And half and half.

    —EUGENE L. SHIRK,
        former cross-country coach at Albright College in Reading,
           Pennsylvania, who at age 91 was the oldest college coach in
           any sport in the country,
        as quoted in *December Champions* by Bob Darden and W.R.
           Spence, M.D., 1993

Football

A game that requires the constant conjuring of animosity.

— VINCE LOMBARDI,
    legendary coach of the Green Bay Packers and Washington
        Redskins,
    referring to the game of football, as quoted in the *New York
        Times*, December 10, 1967

Some people try to find things in this game that don't exist, but
football is only two things—blocking and tackling.

— VINCE LOMBARDI,
    legendary coach of the Green Bay Packers and Washington
        Redskins,
    as recalled upon his death

The nice aspect about it [football] is that, if things go wrong, it's
the manager who gets the blame.

— GARY LINEKER,
    English football player,
    a remark made before his first match as captain of England,
    as quoted in the *Independent* on September 12, 1990

Pro football is like nuclear warfare. There are no winners, only sur-
vivors.

— FRANK GIFFORD,
    former New York Giants halfback and Hall of Famer turned
        broadcaster,
    as quoted in *Sports Illustrated*, July 4, 1960

Football is not a contact sport. Football is a collision sport. Danc-
ing is a contact sport.

— DUFFY DAUGHERTY,
    head football coach at Michigan State University, winner of
        the national title in 1965,
    as quoted in the *The Book of Football Wisdom*, edited by
        Criswell Freeman, 1996

Some people think football is a matter of life and death . . . I can assure them it is much more serious than that.

→ BILL SHANKLY,
Scottish football player and club manager,
as quoted in the *Sunday Times* on Oct. 4, 1981

Three things can happen when you put a [foot]ball in the air—and two of them are bad.

→ DUFFY DAUGHERTY,
head football coach at Michigan State University, winner of
the national title in 1965,
as quoted in the *The Book of Football Wisdom*, edited by
Criswell Freeman, 1996

Football is a game played with arms, legs and shoulders but mostly from the neck up.

→ KNUTE ROCKNE,
legendary college football coach who's credited with establishing Notre Dame as a football powerhouse,
from *The Speaker's Electronic Reference Collection*, AApex
Software, 1994

Football is an honest game. It's true to life. It's a game about shar-
ing. Football is a team game. So is life.

→ JOE NAMATH,
Hall of Fame quarterback, also known as "Broadway Joe,"
as quoted in *The Book of Football Wisdom*, edited by Criswell
Freeman, 1996

It was an ideal day for football—too cold for the spectators and too cold for the players.

→ RED SMITH,
legendary sportswriter,
reporting on a game in 1963 between the Chicago Bears and
the New York Giants

Don't worry about it. It's just a bunch of guys with an odd-shaped ball.

→ BILL PARCELLS,
former coach of the New York Giants, New England Patriots
and New York Jets,
as quoted in *New York* magazine, January 26, 1987

Football is a game of cliches, and I believe in every one of them.

    ◆─VINCE LOMBARDI,
        legendary coach of the Green Bay Packers and Washington
           Redskins,
        as quoted in *The Speaker's Electronic Reference Collection*,
           AApex Software, 1994

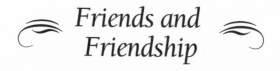

Friends and Friendship

You find out who your friends are. Some people didn't have much to do with me when I was down. I've got a long memory.

    ◆─LANNY WADKINS,
        professional golfer,
        as quoted in *Golfers on Golf*, edited by Downs MacRury, 1979

Golfers are automatically friends. I can feel comfortable and take intense pleasure playing golf with a President—or a young fellow who supports himself as a busboy.

    ◆─ARNOLD PALMER,
        Hall of Fame golfer,
        as quoted in *Golfers on Golf*, edited by Downs MacRury, 1979

Fun

I'm not going to change my life for anybody. I just want to be the best and do it in my own little way. Drink a few beers and have fun.

    ◆─IAN WOOSNAM,
        professional golfer,
        as quoted in *Golfers on Golf*, edited by Downs MacRury, 1979

The players are too serious. They don't have any fun any more. They come to camp with a financial adviser and they read the stock market page before the sports pages. They concern themselves with statistics rather than simply playing the game and enjoying it for what it is. Sure, I've got a job to do, but I also try to give them a little humor. They play better when they relax, and when they play better I can relax.

—ROCKY BRIDGES,
former major league manager,
as quoted in *The Sporting News*, December 12, 1970

It's supposed to be fun. The man says "Play ball," not "Work ball," you know . . . You only have a few years to play this game, and you can't play it if you're all tied up in knots.

—WILLIE STARGELL,
Hall of Fame first baseman for the Pittsburgh Pirates,
as quoted in *Late Innings* by Roger Angell, 1982

Whenever I pitch during the regular season, it's work. To me, it's a routine thing, like going to the office or walking into a factory. You have a job to do and you go out and try to do it. But the play-offs, the World Series and things like the All-Star Game are just plain fun.

—DON SUTTON,
Hall of Fame pitcher with the Los Angeles Dodgers, Houston
Astros, Milwaukee Brewers, Oakland Athletics, and California Angels, who later became a broadcaster,
as quoted in the *Los Angeles Times*, October 6, 1978

I'm still in the same mode of trying to win championships, and at the same time, I'm trying to have fun, too. Everything is fun. I played for fun for nine straight years. We happened to win championships.

—MICHAEL JORDAN,
former NBA basketball superstar with the Chicago Bulls,
after returning to the NBA after his first "retirement,"
as quoted in the *Chicago Tribune*, March 20, 1995

The essence of the game is not "fun," but the soul-satisfying awareness that comes from communal work and sacrifice.

    ◄—RED BLAIK,
        legendary coach of Army's football team during the 1940s,
        as quoted in *The Book of Football Wisdom*, edited by Criswell
           Freeman, 1996

Gambling

I do not think I exaggerate one bit when I say that legalization (of gambling) could jeopardize the very existence of professional baseball and other professional team sports. It is our position that any form of gambling on professional baseball games, legal or illegal, poses a threat to the integrity of our game, exposes it to grave economic danger, and threatens a disservice to the public interest.

    ◄—BOWIE KUHN,
        former major league baseball commissioner,
        testifying before the National Gambling Commission in
           February 1975

I want to establish that I don't have a problem and that I'm in control of my life financially, emotionally and physically, and I felt the reports were kind of misleading in that sense.

    ◄—MICHAEL JORDAN,
        former NBA superstar with the Chicago Bulls,
        responding to allegations that he had a gambling problem,
        as quoted in *Michael Jordan Speaks* by Janet Lowe

They (my family) never came to me and said, "Michael, you have a gambling problem." My wife never said anything, and she's the chief of finances in our household.

    ◄—MICHAEL JORDAN,
        former NBA superstar with the Chicago Bulls,
        responding to allegations that he had a gambling problem,
        as quoted in *Michael Jordan Speaks* by Janet Lowe

Giving Back

It's not about money, it's something I always wanted to do. It's a lot of fun. I want to give back to the community. I got a warmer welcome here than I did when I was drafted.

> —RANDAL "THRILL" HILL,
> former Miami Dolphins receiver,
> talking about his new job as a policeman in Sunrise, Florida.
> The starting salary for the law enforcement job is $35,789,
> compared to the $950,000 Hill got when he was drafted by
> the Dolphins.
> As quoted in *The Pittsburgh Post Gazette*, December 31, 1999

From what we get, we can make a living. What we give, however, makes a life.

> —ARTHUR ASHE,
> Hall of Fame tennis player and AIDS activist,
> as quoted in *Days of Grace*

My dad has always taught me these words: care and share. That's why we put on clinics. The only thing I can do is try to give back. If it works, it works.

> —TIGER WOODS,
> professional golfer,
> from "An Interview with Tiger Woods," on www.golf.com

I have been involved in my community in volunteerism, so I'm very high on helping other folks. It gives me optimism for humankind to see folks helping one another. And how nice it was to learn that one can get endorphins when you help other people! It's the same high as runner's high, but you only get it from a face-to-face situation, not by just writing a check. How nice it is to be rewarded for doing something we ought to be doing anyhow.

> —RORY SPARROW,
> former NBA player and one of *Sports Illustrated's* Sportsmen
> of the Year in 1987,
> encouraging the youth he volunteers to help

Service to others is the rent you pay for your room here on earth.

—MUHAMMAD ALI,
　Olympic gold medalist and former heavyweight champion of
　　the world,
　in *The Greatest* by Muhammad Ali, with Richard Durham,
　　1975

Glory

The great fallacy is that the game is first and last about winning. It's
nothing of the kind. The game is about glory. It's about doing
things in style, with a flourish, about going out and beating the
other lot, not waiting for them to die of boredom.

—DANNY BLANCHFLOWER,
　Northern Ireland-born football player,
　as quoted in *The Glory Game* by Hunter Davis, 1972

Goals and Objectives

It's a challenge, just like business has been. Getting out there, trying to win. To me, winning isn't the only thing, it's everything. If
that's your goal, go for it. If it is starting out in business and having
a goal of making a million dollars—I believe if you work hard
enough at it, whatever it is, it'll come.

—JOHN T. OXLEY,
　polo player,
　explaining why he was still playing at age 83,
　as quoted in *December Champions* by Bob Darden and W.R.
　　Spence, M.D., 1993

Before I was ever in my teens, I knew exactly what I wanted to be when I grew up. My goal was to be the greatest athlete that ever lived.

➤ BABE DIDRIKSON ZAHARIAS,
  Hall of Fame golfer, sportswoman, and Olympic champion,
  in the *Ultimate Success Quotations Library*, Cyber Nation
    International, Inc., Reno, NV, 1997

We have one goal and one goal only—and that's to win the Stanley Cup.

➤ WAYNE GRETZKY,
  NHL superstar,
  as quoted in *The Great One: The Life and Times of Wayne
    Gretzky* by Andrew Podnieks, 1999

You can't climb up to the second floor without a ladder. When you set your aim too high and don't fulfill it, then your enthusiasm turns to bitterness. Try for a goal that's reasonable, and then gradually raise it. That's the only way to get to the top.

➤ EMIL ZANTOPEK,
  Czech athlete, middle-distance runner, and gold medal winner
    in the 1948 and 1952 Olympics,
  as quoted in *The Guinness Dictionary of Sports Quotations*
    by Colin Jarman, 1990.

Many people flounder about in life because they have no purpose. Before it is possible to achieve anything, an objective must be set.

➤ GEORGE HALAS,
  legendary Hall of Fame coach of the Chicago Bears and a
    charter member of the Hall of Fame,
  as quoted in *The Book of Football Wisdom*, edited by Criswell
    Freeman, 1996

 God and Religion

You pay a price for the killer instinct. I don't care who you are, but you pay a price for that in our culture. Our economic philosophy of capitalism and our Christian ethics are complete polar opposites. We go to church on Sunday morning and are told to turn the other cheek, be a nice boy and practice everything else in the Old and New Testament. Capitalism is exactly the opposite—it's every man for himself. We're rewarded according to how much we produce and we can only "win through intimidation." Remember the Lombardi theory—look out for Number One.

> ⎯ARTHUR ASHE,
> Hall of Fame tennis player and AIDS activist,
> in his book *Off the Court*, with Neil Amdur, 1981

Football is like a religion to me. I worship the ball, and I treat it like a god. Too many players think of a football as something to kick. They should be taught to caress it and to treat it like a precious gem.

> ⎯PELE,
> Brazilian soccer player, one of the greatest of all time,
> as quoted in *The Cassell Soccer Companion* by David
> Pickering, 1994

My religious faith is very, very important to me in all of my decisions in life. It is my life. I don't know what I would do without it. I would have no outlet. I'm now nearing the end of my life at 96. If I had no hope for the future, what would I do?

> ⎯HULDA CROOKS,
> a Loma Linda, California, grandmother, who at age 91
> climbed the 14,494-foot Mount Whitney for the twenty-
> third time,
> as quoted in *December Champions* by Bob Darden and W.R.
> Spence, M.D., 1993

A man once told me to walk with the Lord. I'd rather walk with the bases loaded.

> ━ KEN SINGLETON,
>   former major league baseball player turned broadcaster,
>   after forcing in a run with a walk in the 1983 World Series,
>   as quoted in *Baseball's Greatest Quotations*, by Paul Dickson,
>   1991

Everything went well tonight. I thank God for it.

> ━ MICHELLE KWAN,
>   figure skating champion,
>   after winning the 1996 World Championships in Edmonton,
>   Canada,
>   as quoted in *Born to Skate: The Michelle Kwan Story* by
>   Edward Z. Epstein, 1997

I love the warm, welcoming feeling I get from attending Mass. Church helps me feel grounded—even when I'm constantly jetting off to competitions and appearances.

> ━ TARA LIPINSKI,
>   Olympic gold medalist and world figure skating champion,
>   in her autobiography, *Tara Lipinski: Triumph on Ice*, with
>   Emily Costello, 1998

God was Russian tonight.

> ━ SERGE SAVARD,
>   defenseman for the Montreal Canadiens,
>   after losing to the Soviet Red Army hockey team on December
>   31, 1975

Your Holiness, I'm Joseph Medwick. I, too, used to be a Cardinal.

> ━ JOSEPH "DUCKY" MEDWICK,
>   former St. Louis Cardinal outfielder,
>   to the Pope during a visit to the Vatican with a group of
>   servicemen during World War II

Golf

No other game combines the wonder of nature with the discipline of sport in such carefully planned ways. A great golf course both frees and challenges a golfer's mind.

> ➤ TOM WATSON,
>   Hall of Fame golfer,
>   in *The Golfer's Book of Wisdom*, edited by Criswell Freeman, 1995

You know those two-foot downhill putts with a break? I'd rather see a rattlesnake.

> ➤ SAM SNEAD,
>   Hall of Fame golfer and winner of a record 81 Professional Golf Association tournaments,
>   as quoted in *The Golfer's Book of Wisdom*, edited by Criswell Freeman, 1995

Golf has probably kept more people sane than psychiatrists have.

> ➤ HARVEY PENICK,
>   legendary golf instructor,
>   as quoted in *The Golfer's Book of Wisdom*, edited by Criswell Freeman, 1995

Golf is a game that is played on a five-inch course—the distance between your ears.

> ➤ BOBBY JONES,
>   Hall of Fame golfer and four-time winner of the U.S. Open,
>   as quoted in *The Guinness Dictionary of Sports Quotations* by Colin Jarman, 1990.

Golf puts a man's character on the anvil and his richest qualities—patience, poise, and restraint—to the flame.

> ➤ BILLY CASPER,
>   Hall of Fame golfer,
>   as quoted in *The Golfer's Book of Wisdom*, edited by Criswell Freeman, 1995

Golf is the only sport where the ball doesn't move until you hit it.

━TED WILLIAMS,
  legendary Boston Red Sox outfielder and Hall of Famer,
  as quoted in *The Golfer's Book of Wisdom*, edited by Criswell
    Freeman, 1995

Golf is not a funeral, though both can be very sad affairs.

━BERNARD DARWIN,
  professional golfer,
  as quoted in *Golfers on Golf*, edited by Downs MacRury, 1997

When you play for fun, it's fun. But when you play golf for a living, it's a game of sorrows. You're never happy.

━GARY PLAYER,
  Hall of Fame golfer,
  as quoted in *Golfers on Golf*, edited by Downs MacRury, 1997

Golf is not and never has been a fair game.

━JACK NICKLAUS,
  Hall of Fame golfer and winner of 20 major championships,
  as quoted in *The Guinness Dictionary of Sports Quotations*
    by Colin Jarman, 1990

Do your best, one shot at a time and then move on. Remember that golf is just a game.

━NANCY LOPEZ,
  Hall of Fame golfer,
  as quoted in *The Golfer's Book of Wisdom*, edited by Criswell
    Freeman, 1995

Golf is a puzzle without an answer.

━GARY PLAYER,
  Hall of Fame golfer,
  as quoted in *Golfers on Golf*, edited by Downs MacRury, 1997

Golf is a game you never can get too good in. You can improve, but you never can get to where you master the game.

━GAY BREWER,
  professional golfer,
  as quoted in *Golfers on Golf*, edited by Downs MacRury, 1997

Baseball may be a game of inches, as they say, but golf is a game of millimeters.

➤ ARNOLD PALMER,
Hall of Fame golfer,
as quoted in *Golfers on Golf*, edited by Downs MacRury, 1997

Golf asks something of a man. It makes one loathe mediocrity. It seems to say, "If you are going to keep company with me, don't embarrass me."

➤ GARY PLAYER,
Hall of Fame golfer,
as quoted in the *Christian Science Monitor*, June 24, 1965

Golf is a spiritual game. It's like Zen. You have to let your mind take over.

➤ AMY ALCOTT,
Hall of Fame golfer,
as quoted in *The Golfer's Book of Wisdom* edited by Criswell
Freeman, 1995

Golf is a matter of confidence. If you think you cannot do it, there is no chance you will.

➤ HENRY COTTON,
English golfer,
as quoted in *The Golfer's Book of Wisdom*, edited by Criswell
Freeman, 1995

Greed

There are things about some professional athletes that I cannot stand—the pretense, the egos, the pomposity, the greed.

➤ TED SIMMONS,
former major league catcher,
widely quoted

First the players want a hamburger, and the owners gave them a hamburger. Then they wanted a filet mignon, and they gave them a filet mignon. Then they wanted the whole damn cow, and now that they got the cow they want a pasture to put him in. You just can't satisfy them, and I have no sympathy for any of them.

> ──Rip Sewell,
> **former pitcher for the Pittsburgh Pirates,**
> **referring to the greed of current players,**
> **widely quoted**

Happiness

Six Rules for a Happy Life
1. Avoid fried meats which angry up the blood
2. If your stomach disputes you, lie down and pacify it with cool thoughts
3. Keep the juices flowing by jangling around gently as you move
4. Go very light on vices such as carrying on in society. The social ramble ain't restful
5. Avoid running at all times
6. Don't look back. Something may be gaining on you

> ──Satchel Paige,
> **superstar pitcher in the Negro Leagues and one of the first**
> **African-Americans to play in the major leagues.**
> **Paige had these rules inscribed on business cards, which he**
> **would pass out to fans.**

The best way to forget one's self is to look at the world with attention and love.

> ──Red Auerbach,
> **legendary Hall of Fame basketball coach who led the Boston**
> **Celtics to nine NBA championships,**
> **as quoted in *The Ultimate Success Quotations Library*, Cyber**
> **Nation International, Inc., Reno, NV, 1997**

My secret is to smoke six or seven cigars, enjoy a little wine at night, have a beautiful wife who loves you, and have a great caddie like mine, that's all.

➤ LARRY LAORETTI,
    professional golfer,
    as quoted in *Golfers on Golf*, edited by Downs MacRury, 1997

 *Heroes*

Kids today are looking for idols, but sometimes they look too far . . . They don't have to look any farther than their home because those are the people that love you. They are the real heroes.

➤ BOBBY BONILLA,
    major league baseball player,
    as quoted in *USA Today*, March 30, 1989

I play for the poor man. I try to give a thrill to the lunch bucket fan. I know their plight. I worked in a factory in high school. The poor folk who lay out the hard bread to see a game. That's where my heart lies. The rich don't need heroes.

➤ LEON WAGNER,
    former major league baseball player,
    as quoted in *Baseball Digest*, April 1968

He has created an expectation of hero worship on the part of the youth of this country, and it was a most fortunate thing that (Babe) Ruth kept faith with the boyhood of America because they loved him.

➤ BRANCH RICKEY,
    major league baseball innovator and president-general man-
        ager of the Brooklyn Dodgers, who integrated professional
        baseball in 1947 by bringing up Jackie Robinson; referring
        to Babe Ruth,
    as quoted in the *San Francisco Examiner* in observance of the
        twentieth anniversary of Ruth's death in 1968

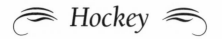 *Hockey*

I played hockey at Norwood High School in Boston. We'd have 15,000 for some games in the Boston Arena. I was hit on the mouth three times. I was hit by a puck. That cost me a tooth and a half. The half-tooth had the nerve exposed. That's the worst pain I ever felt. But I had them broken twice more. I was hit in a head-on collision and again with a stick in the same place. Then I was hit with a puck on the chin. Twenty stitches. You're better off in baseball.

➤ RICHIE HEBNER,
  former major league baseball player,
  explaining why he chose baseball instead of hockey,
  as quoted in *Baseball Digest*, August 1969

The severity of injuries on a pain scale doesn't compare in baseball and hockey. If you talked to a hockey player about having a bone spur or a bone chip, he'd laugh.

➤ KIRK MCCASKILL,
  former major league pitcher,
  as quoted in the *Washington Times* on August 20, 1990, when
    he was a collegiate All-American hockey player at the
    University of Vermont

This fastest of games (hockey) has become almost as much of a national symbol as the maple leaf.

➤ LESTER B. PEARSON,
  prime minister of Canada,
  as quoted in 1968

Home Runs

Hitting a home run is a great feeling—it gives you a big charge. You know that's what the people like to see. It's what you guys (sportswriters) like to see, too. Just stop and think how you rush up to the home run hitters after every game. With all that glamour attached to hitting the ball out of the park, it takes a lot of discipline to go up there and just try to get a hit.

> —GARRY MADDOX,
> former major league outfielder,
> as quoted in the *Christian Science Monitor*, April 25, 1977

I get on base by making good contact with the ball, but whenever I hit a home run I'm as surprised as everybody else.

> —AMOS OTIS,
> former major league player with the Kansas City Royals,
> as quoted in the *Christian Science Monitor*, October 13,
> 1978

Human Spirit

In the end we are all part of the same deal. We try to beat each other's brains out, but we know each other's families and we share the same hopes and dreams. We're closer than we know.

> —LANNY WADKINS,
> professional golfer,
> speaking about the great turnout of golfers at Payne Stewart's
> funeral and the unspoken bond between golfers

The only bond worth anything between human beings is their humanness.

> ⟶JESSE OWENS,
>> the greatest sprinter of his generation and the winner of four
>> gold medals at the Berlin Olympics in 1936,
>> from an Internet collection of quotations

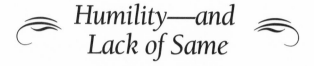

Humility—and Lack of Same

You know, this team . . . it all flows from me. I've got to keep it going. I'm the straw that stirs the drink . . . [Thurman] Munson thinks he can be the straw that stirs the drink, but he can only stir it bad. The rest of the guys should know that I don't feel far above them . . . I mean, nobody can turn people on like I can, or do for a club the things I can do, but we are still athletes, we're all still ballplayers.

> ⟶REGGIE JACKSON,
>> former New York Yankees outfielder,
>> as remarked during spring training in May 1977 with the New
>> York Yankees and quoted in *Sport*, June 1977; Jackson
>> denied the quotes.

They tried to get a Cadillac for the price of a Chevy.

> ⟶COREY DILLON,
>> Cincinnati Bengals running back,
>> on the team's $18 million contract offer, which he rejected

I am the greatest!

> ⟶MUHAMMAD ALI,
>> Olympic gold medalist and former world heavyweight
>> champion,
>> as quoted in the *Louisville Times*, November 16, 1962

I'm not the greatest; I'm the double greatest. Not only do I knock 'em out, I pick the round.

> ➤MUHAMMAD ALI,
> Olympic gold medalist and former world heavyweight champion,
> as quoted in the *New York Times*, December 9, 1962

Superman don't need no seat belt.

> ➤MUHAMMAD ALI,
> Olympic gold medalist and former world heavyweight champion,
> commenting to an airline attendant who replied, "Superman don't need no airplane, either."

I am the best in baseball. This may sound conceited, but I want to be honest about how I feel . . . there is no one who does as many things as well as I do . . . I can do it all and I create an excitement in a ballpark when I walk on the field.

> ➤REGGIE JACKSON,
> former Oakland Athletics and New York Yankees outfielder,
> from *Reggie: A Season with a Superstar* by Reggie Jackson with Bill Libby, 1975

I'm the best. I just haven't played yet.

> ➤MUHAMMAD ALI,
> Olympic gold medalist and former world heavyweight champion,
> when asked about the quality of his golf game

It's bloody tough being a legend.

> ➤RON ATKINSON,
> English football player and manager,
> as quoted in *The Book of Football Quotations* by Peter Ball and Phil Shaw, 1989

At home I am a nice guy, but I don't want the world to know. Humble people, I've found, don't get very far.

> ➤MUHAMMAD ALI,
> Olympic gold medalist and former world heavyweight champion,
> as quoted in the *Sunday Express*, January 13, 1963

I can't think of anything more humiliating than losing a ballgame to a guy who steals home on you. It happened to me one time against Kansas City. I had a 2-and-2 count on the hitter—and Amos Otis broke from third. The pitch was a ball and he slid in safe. I felt like a nickel.

➤ NOLAN RYAN,
   Hall of Fame pitcher and the all-time leader in strikeouts,
   as quoted in the *Los Angeles Herald-Examiner*, July 13,
      1977

Humor

The problem with having a sense of humor is often that people you use it on aren't in a very good mood.

➤ LOU HOLTZ,
   longtime college football coach,
   as quoted in *Sports Illustrated*, December 9, 1985

Keep your sense of humor. There's enough stress in the rest of your life to let bad shots ruin a game you're supposed to enjoy.

➤ AMY ALCOTT,
   Hall of Fame golfer,
   as quoted in *Golfers on Golf*, edited by Downs MacRury,
      1997

You need two things to be a good one—a sense of humor and a bullpen.

➤ WHITEY HERZOG,
   former major league manager,
   from *The Whitey Herzog Quote Machine*, which appeared in
      the *St. Louis Post-Dispatch* when Herzog resigned as
      Cardinals manager

Image

I'm projected as something that's horrible, and it's very, very uncomfortable. I try to give of myself and do things for people, and to be spit at and thrown at and cursed at is a very uncomfortable thing. . . . [I]t's hard to play when somebody says you're no good or somebody says you can't do this or you can't do that or you're a lousy person or you're greedy or egotistical. Those things are tough and unfair. I'm human. I've played my butt off for 10 years. I'm not a loafer. I'm not a jerk. I'm a baseball player. That's what I want to do. I don't want to get famous. If I deserve it with my bat, give me credit. If I don't, leave me be.

➣ REGGIE JACKSON,
former New York Yankees outfielder,
talking about what it was like to play with the Yankees,
as quoted in the *Dallas Times-Herald*, August 27, 1978

Improvement

The principle is competing against yourself. It's about self-improvement, about being better than you were the day before.

➣ STEVE YOUNG,
San Francisco 49ers quarterback,
as quoted in *Get Lost Adventure Magazine*

We have a saying in Russia. Each soldier desires to be a general. If you don't want to work to be a general, why are you here?

➣ IRINA RODNINA,
Russian former championship figure skater and skating
coach,
as quoted in *Born to Skate: The Michelle Kwan Story* by
Edward Z. Epstein, 1997

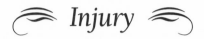 *Injury*

I was X-rayed so often I glowed in the dark.

➤ BILLY GRABARKETWITZ,
former Los Angeles Dodgers third baseman,
recalling the series of broken bones he suffered while playing
in the minor leagues in 1968,
as quoted in *The Sporting News*, June 27, 1970

I've never been hurt by a ground ball, and yet I've got more false
teeth than a Polish fullback. Funny isn't it?

➤ BROOKS ROBINSON,
Hall of Fame third baseman with the Baltimore Orioles
turned broadcaster,
after breaking two teeth when he lost control of a bat in a
batting cage, and the bat bounced off the side of the cage
and hit him in the mouth,
as quoted in *Sport Magazine's All-time All Stars*, edited by Tom
Murray, 1977

My body could stand the crutches but my mind couldn't stand the
sideline.

➤ MICHAEL JORDAN,
former NBA superstar with the Chicago Bulls,
referring to a broken bone in his foot that sidelined him for
64 games during the 1985 to 1986 season,
as quoted in *Newsweek*, January 5, 1987

A fellow was playing with long reins and the toe of my boot jerked
the reins out of his hands. He jerked them back up into the air, and
I fell six and a half feet. I broke seven ribs—the top one in two
places—punctured my right lung, pinched a nerve in my shoulder,
and later developed a nerve problem in my right hand. It took me
three or four months to get over all of that.

➤ JOHN T. OXLEY,
polo player,
describing an accident he had while playing in 1990 at age 80,
as quoted in *December Champions* by Bob Darden and W.R.
Spence, M.D., 1993

Sooner or later the arm goes bad. It has to. The arm wasn't meant to stand the strain pitching imposes on it. Sooner or later, you have to start pitching in pain.

➤WHITEY FORD,
   Hall of Fame pitcher for the New York Yankees,
   as quoted in *Vida: His Own Story* by Bill Libby and Vida Blue,
      1972

I walk into the clubhouse, and it's like walking into the Mayo Clinic. We have four doctors, three therapists and five trainers. Back when I broke in, we had one trainer, who carried a bottle of rubbing alcohol—and by the seventh inning he had drunk it all.

➤TOMMY LASORDA,
   former Los Angeles Dodgers manager,
   referring to the treatment of injuries,
   as quoted in *Sports Illustrated*, May 29, 1989

It has to be physical. That's why I'm soaking my arm now. If it was mental, I'd be soaking my head!

➤JIM LONBORG,
   former major league pitcher,
   when asked if the difficulty he had pitching after only two
      days of rest was due to physical or mental reasons,
   as quoted *in Baseball Digest*, January 1968

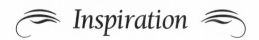 *Inspiration*

Some time, Rock, when the team's up against it, when things are wrong and the breaks are beating the boys—tell them to go in there with all they've got and win just one for the Gipper.

➤GEORGE GIPP,
   American football player who died of pneumonia at age 25.
   These were his last words to his Notre Dame coach Knute
      Rockne, who later repeated Gipp's words to his team,
      inspiring them to win. The phrase "Win one for the
      Gipper" became common.

Jet Lag

But there's nothing you can do for jet lag except get down to an event early and let it run its course like a good virus.

> ─ANDRE AGASSI,
>> professional tennis player and winner of six major championships,
>> as quoted on ESPNet SportsZone

Actually, the trip here isn't bad for me as far as the flight and time change. You leave at night from L.A. and sleep on the flight and you get here. When I go from West to East it isn't too bad. I always have trouble going over to Europe with the time change, but coming to Australia, Asia is really not a problem. Going back is another issue. One year it took me about a week to recover, from my appetite to my sleeping, because you just get used to this time and then it's tough going back.

> ─PETE SAMPRAS,
>> professional tennis player and winner of 12 major championships,
>> referring to traveling between the United States and Australia,
>> as quoted on *ESPNet SportsZone*

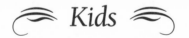

Kids

I think too many adults, if they go visit a family, spend all their time talking with the other adults while the poor children don't get much attention. They love them, but they don't spend that much time with them. I spend my time with the grandchildren and let the adults talk!

> ─EUGENE L. SHIRK,
>> former crosscountry coach at Albright College in Reading, Pennsylvania, who at age 91 was the oldest college coach in any sport in the country,
>> as quoted in *December Champions* by Bob Darden and W.R. Spence, M.D., 1993

Sure, kids need capable instruction and coaching, but not when they're 10 or 11 years old. Say the boy starts going to football camp when he is 10. He goes every summer and a lot of time, energy, effort and money are spent to make him a football or a basketball player. By the time he reaches his senior year in high school, he must be pretty darn sick of it all and he gets to feel that it's almost a chore. That he has been doing this same thing for seven or eight years. I don't think, psychologically, that's good for any youngster. It deprives him of a chance to perhaps do what he really wanted to do. Like playing the piano or maybe milking cows. I think we ought to let go of our kids. If they get interested in a sport, fine, but let them do it on their own. Don't impose it on them, don't have an organized program.

➤JOE PATERNO,
   longtime football coach at Penn State,
   as quoted in *Joe Paterno: Football My Way* by Mervin D.
   Hyman and Gordon S. White Jr., 1978

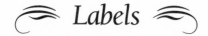 *Labels*

I came to live in a country I love; some people label me a defector. I have loved men and women in my life; I've been labeled "the bisexual defector." Want to know another secret? I'm even ambidextrous. I don't like labels. Just call me Martina.

➤MARTINA NAVRATILOVA,
   Hall of Fame tennis player,
   from her book *Martina Navratilova: Being Myself*, 1985

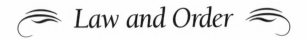

Law and Order

From now on I intend to organize my own law out there in right field. From now on any fan who thinks he has a license to use bad language in the right field bleachers is going to get a fine surprise. Anybody who thinks he gets the privilege of calling me all sorts of nasty names when he pays 50 cents to go into the bleachers is in for another thought. If any fan in the future uses indecent language, either to me or any other Yankee, I will stop the game, call a policeman, and have the fan thrown out of the park. I am going to be my own law from now on.

➤ BABE RUTH,
   legendary Hall of Fame baseball player,
   as quoted in the *New York Telegram*, May 30, 1929

Foremost, we must recognize that there are two people here: Peter Rose, the living legend, the all-time hit leader, and the idol of millions; and Pete Rose, the individual, who appears today convicted of two counts of cheating on his taxes. Today, we are not dealing with the legend . . .

➤ JUDGE ARTHUR S. SPIEGEL,
   just before sentencing Pete Rose to serve five months in
      prison for tax evasion

The cops picked me up on the street at 3 a.m. and fined me $500 for being drunk and $100 for being with the Phillies.

➤ BOB UECKER,
   former major league catcher, turned broadcaster,
   recalling the time he spent as a Philadelphia Phillie in 1966
      and 1967,
   as quoted in *The Sporting News*, September 26, 1988

Leadership

Part of being a leader means knowing who you can go after and who you should pat on the butt.

  —GARY PAYTON,
    Seattle SuperSonics point guard,
    discussing his role on his team,
    as quoted in *Sports Illustrated*, December 20, 1999

Maybe they made me captain because I've been here so long. But if I'm supposed to be captain by example, I'll be a terrible captain.

  —THURMAN MUNSON,
    New York Yankees catcher.
    This 1976 quote was used in his obituary by the Associated
      Press after Munson was killed in a plane crash in 1979.

Leadership is a matter of having people look at you and gain confidence, seeing how you react. If you're in control, they're in control.

  —TOM LANDRY,
    legendary Dallas Cowboys coach from 1960 to 1988 and win-
      ner of two Super Bowls,
    from *The Ultimate Success Quotations Library*, Cyber Nation
      International, Inc., Reno, NV, 1997

To be a leader, you have to make people want to follow you, and nobody wants to follow someone who doesn't know where he is going.

  —JOE NAMATH,
    Hall of Fame quarterback,
    in *The Ultimate Success Quotations Library*, Cyber Nation
      International, Inc., Reno, NV, 1997

Good fellows are a dime a dozen, but an aggressive leader is priceless.

  —RED BLAIK,
    legendary Army football coach during the 1940s,
    as quoted in *The Book of Football Wisdom*, edited by Criswell
      Freeman, 1996

If no one wants to assume that role as leader, then our team's not going to go very far.

—DeMarco Farr,
St. Louis Rams linebacker,
speaking about the team's lack of leadership in the past,
as quoted in the *Contra Costa Times,* January 1, 2000

Learning

The important thing is to learn a lesson every time you lose. Life is a learning process and you have to try to learn what's best for you. Let me tell you, life is not fun when you're banging your head against a brick wall all the time.

—John McEnroe,
Hall of Fame tennis player, U.S. Davis Cup captain and broadcaster,
in *Words of Wisdom* by William Safire and Leonard Safire, 1989

This taught me a lesson, but I'm not sure what it is.

—John McEnroe,
Hall of Fame tennis player, U.S. Davis Cup captain and broadcaster,
on losing to Tim Mayotte in the Ebel U.S. Pro Indoor Championships,
as quoted in the *New York Times*, February 9, 1987

I wish I'd known early what I had to learn late.

—Richie Ashburn,
Hall of Fame center fielder for the Philadelphia Phillies, Chicago Cubs, and New York Mets,
talking about the fact that when he was young, he was so fast that he didn't have to learn to hit,
as quoted in *Late Innings* by Roger Angell, 1982

The best and fastest way to learn a sport is to watch and imitate a champion.

➤ JEAN-CLAUDE KILLY,
Olympic gold medalist skier,
as quoted in *Get Lost Adventure Magazine*

It's what you learn after you know it all that counts.

➤ EARL WEAVER,
Hall of Fame manager of the Baltimore Orioles
said in 1968, as widely quoted

You can learn little from victory. You can learn everything from defeat.

➤ CHRISTY MATHEWSON,
Hall of Fame pitcher,
as quoted in *The Tumult and the Shouting* by Grantland Rice,
1954

Some people are so busy learning the tricks of the trade that they never learn the trade.

➤ VERNON LAW,
former pitcher for the Pittsburgh Pirates,
as quoted in *This Week*, August 14, 1960

We live and learn, and big mountains are stern teachers.

➤ BILL TILMAN,
English mountaineer and sailor,
as quoted in his book, *Two Mountains and a River*, 1949

 *Life*

Life is a precious thing. One day it's going to slip out from under you, and you're not going to be here.

➤ BRIAN GAMBLE,
  Texas A&M linebacker,
  after the collapse of a bonfire construction site on November
  18, 1999, at Texas A&M that killed 12 people

 *Lifestyles*

When I come back in the next life, I want to come back as a golf pro's wife. She wakes up every morning at crack of 10 and is faced by her first major decision of the day: whether to have breakfast in bed or in the hotel coffee shop.

➤ DON SIKES,
  professional golfer,
  as quoted in *Golfers on Golf*, edited by Downs MacRury, 1997

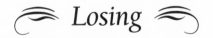 *Losing*

Show me a good loser and I'll show you an idiot.

➤ LEO DUROCHER,
  Hall of Fame manager of the Brooklyn Dodgers and New York
  Giants,
  attributed

The depth of anguish I felt after every loss over the past few years has begun to reach an intensity that the thrill of victory couldn't overcome.

➤MARV LEVY,
former head coach of the Buffalo Bills,
referring to the Bills' losses in four consecutive Super Bowls

We can't win at home. We can't win on the road. As general manager, I just can't figure out where else to play.

➤PAT WILLIAMS,
general manager of the Orlando Magic,
referring to his team's 7-27 record in 1992,
as quoted on the Success For You.net website

Losing is easy. It's not enjoyable, but it's easy.

➤BUD WILKINSON,
legendary Hall of Fame football coach at the University of
Oklahoma from 1947 to 1963; won three national championships,
as quoted in *The Book of Football Wisdom*, edited by Criswell
Freeman, 1996

The first thing I do after losing, regardless of whether I lost a close one because of a silly lapse or simply was snowed under by a rival running on a hot streak, is to forget it. I take a look at my calendar and start thinking about where we'll be playing next week, and I'll show 'em then!

➤NANCY LOPEZ,
Hall of Fame golfer,
as quoted in *Golfers On Golf*, edited by Downs MacRury,
1997

If there was a league in this nation that that team could have won in, it has not been brought to my attention. And that includes Little League.

➤PAUL RICHARDS,
general manager of the 1976 Chicago White Sox,
referring to his team's dismal season, as quoted in *Sox: From
Lane and Fain to Zisk and Fisk* by Bob Vanderberg

Fullmer kicked the hell out of me!

    CARMEN BASILIO,
      former middleweight boxer,
      referring to his 1959 middleweight title bout against Gene
        Fullmer

I never thought of losing, but now that it's happened, the only thing is to do it right. That's my obligation to all the people who believe in me. We all have to take defeats in life.

    MUHAMMAD ALI,
      Olympic gold medalist and former world heavyweight cham-
        pion,
      after losing his first fight to Ken Norton on March 31, 1973

If you're old and you lose, they say you're outmoded. If you're young and you lose, they say you're green. So don't lose.

    TERRY BRENNAN,
      former University of Notre Dame football coach,
      as quoted in *Life*, March 1957

 *Loyalty*

I don't think there's any loyalty in baseball at all. It's become such a transient business. If you knew you were going to be with a team 10 years, then you could be loyal to a tradition. But when you know they can get rid of you tomorrow . . .

    GRAIG NETTLES,
      former third baseman with the New York Yankees,
      as quoted in the *Los Angeles Times*, March 23, 1978

I bleed Dodger blue, and when I die, I'm going to the Big Dodger in the sky.

    TOMMY LASORDA,
      former manager of the Los Angeles Dodgers,
      his much-quoted oath of loyalty

Managing and Managers

Sure I played, did you think I was born at the age of 70 sitting in a dugout trying to manage guys like you?

━**CASEY STENGEL,**
    former manager of the New York Yankees and New York
      Mets,
    when asked by Mickey Mantle if he had ever played baseball

The night we won the World Series, I was understandably feeling my oats. I asked my wife how many really great managers she thought there were in baseball. Glaring at me, she said, "I think there's one less than you do."

━**DANNY MURTAUGH,**
    former manager of the Pittsburgh Pirates,
    as quoted in *Sport,* May 1961

From what I've observed, owners don't fire managers merely for losing. They fire them if the public is complaining. In some cases, the public will say it wasn't the manager's fault. But when it blames the manager, the owner feels he has to move, and the lovable old skipper gets thrown out on his can . . . In most cases, the "public" is the press. If the press writes that the fans feel the manager is doing a bad job, that usually means the press feels he's doing a bad job.

━**EARL WEAVER,**
    Hall of Fame manager of the Baltimore Orioles,
    as quoted in the *Los Angeles Herald-Examiner*, April 22,
      1976

I believe if God had ever managed, He would have been very aggressive, the way I manage.

━**BILLY MARTIN,**
    while managing the Oakland A's,
    as quoted in *Sports Illustrated*, March 30, 1981

The toughest thing about managing is standing up for nine innings.

> ← PAUL OWENS,
>> former manager of the Philadelphia Phillies,
>> as quoted in *Sports Illustrated*, October 13, 1973

He can step on your shoes, but he doesn't mess up your shine.

> ← JOE MORGAN,
>> Hall of Fame second baseman, turned broadcaster,
>> on the ability of manager Frank Robinson to criticize players
>>   without alienating them,
>> as quoted in *Sports Illustrated*, July 13, 1981

Managers don't have as much leverage as they used to have. We can't really be the boss. If I say to a veteran player, "If you don't perform, you may be sent back to the minors", they look at me and say: "Who are you kidding? I'm not going anyplace . . . I've already had three years in the major leagues. You can't send me back to the minor leagues without my OK."

> ← FRANK ROBINSON,
>> two-time Triple Crown winner, Hall of Famer and the major
>>   leagues' first African-American manager,
>> as quoted in *Washingtonian*, August 1989

I believe managing is like holding a dove in your hand. If you hold it too tightly, you kill it, but if you hold it too loosely, you lose it.

> ← TOMMY LASORDA,
>> former manager of the Los Angeles Dodgers,
>> from his book *The Artful Dodger*, 1985

Managing is getting paid for home runs someone else runs.

> ← CASEY STENGEL,
>> former manager of the New York Yankees and New York
>>   Mets,
>> recalled on his death, September 29, 1975

Marriage

The most important single qualification a man should have to marry one of my daughters is infinite kindness. Infinite kindness will sustain a marriage through all its problems, its uncertainties, its illnesses, its disappointments, its storms, its tension, its fear, its separations, its sorrows. Out of infinite kindness can grow real love and understanding and tolerance and warmth. Nothing can take the place of such an enduring asset.

> ━BRANCH RICKEY,
> major league baseball innovator and president-general
> manager of the Brooklyn Dodgers,
> as quoted in *Branch Rickey* by Murray Polner, 1983

If each time a player and caddie split up was actually a divorce, most tour players would have been "married" more times than Zsa Zsa and Liz combined.

> ━PETER JACOBSEN,
> professional golfer,
> as quoted in *Golfers on Golf*, edited by Downs MacRury, 1997

My wife doesn't care what I do when I'm away as long as I don't have a good time.

> ━LEE TREVINO,
> Hall of Fame golfer,
> as quoted in *Golfers on Golf*, edited by Downs MacRury, 1997

I'm low if I have a bad round, but at least I know that he still loves me—or I think so.

> ━ANNIKA SORENSTAM,
> professional golfer and two-time U.S. Women's Open
> champion,
> referring to her husband, David Esch,
> as quoted in *Sports Illustrated*, July 21, 1997

I told the writers, if you're going to print anything about us, you can say for the bridegroom that it's the best catch he ever made in his career.

➤ CASEY STENGEL,
former manager of the New York Yankees and New York Mets,
on his marriage in 1942 to actress Edna Lawson

It's no fun being married to an electric light.

➤ JOE DIMAGGIO,
legendary New York Yankees outfielder and Hall of Famer,
on being married to actress Marilyn Monroe

We were happily married for eight months. Unfortunately, we were married for four and a half years.

➤ NICK FALDO,
Hall of Fame golfer,
as quoted in *Golfers on Golf*, edited by Downs MacRury, 1997

When you marry a baseball player, you marry the man, you marry baseball, you marry its rules.

➤ DANIELLE GAGNON TORREZ,
former wife of pitcher Mike Torrez,
in her book *High Inside: Memoirs of a Baseball Wife*, 1993

You've got to time your babies for the offseason and get married in the offseason and get divorced in the offseason. Baseball always comes first.

➤ LIZ MITCHELL,
the wife of baseball player Paul Mitchell,
as quoted in *High Inside: Memoirs of a Baseball Wife* by
Danielle Gagnon Torrez, 1993

It's got to be better than rooming with Joe Paige.

➤ JOE DIMAGGIO,
legendary New York Yankees outfielder and Hall of Famer,
when asked whether being married to Marilyn Monroe would
be good for him

Before I was married, I used to love being alone in a hotel room on the tour, where I don't even have to make my bed, let alone ever cook anything or clean up. Now I feel lonely out there.

> ➤ NANCY LOPEZ,
> Hall of Fame golfer,
> as quoted in *Golfers on Golf*, edited by Downs MacRury, 1997

I just thought about how much I loved her. There was nothing else like it. To have a wife like I have, to be able to share that moment with her.

> ➤ LEE JANZEN,
> professional golfer and two-time U.S. Open champion,
> explaining why he embraced his wife after the 1993 U.S. Open

The Media

I'm trying to figure out what they're doing. I get on a plane in San Diego and they're shooting film. I get off a plane in Cincinnati and they've got another crew from CBS shooting me. After a game, CBS, ABC, NBC are all in here. CBS has been with me something like 68 days. How much footage do they need of a guy?

> ➤ PETE ROSE,
> former major league baseball player and the all-time leader in hits,
> referring to media coverage during the period he was being investigated on gambling charges

I haven't missed a game in two and a half years. I go to the park sick as a dog and, when I see my uniform hanging there, I get well right now. Then I see some of you guys and I get sick again.

> ➤ PETE ROSE,
> professional baseball player and the all-time leader in hits,
> talking to a group of reporters while playing for the Cincinnati Reds

So, no question, I consider the media's scrutiny to be one of intensity, but also an opportunity to learn, to make better decisions for yourself.

— ANDRE AGASSI,
professional tennis player and winner of six major
championships,
talking to reporters about his relationship with the media,
as quoted on ESPNet SportsZone

What's the difference between a 3-week-old puppy and a sportswriter? In 6 weeks, the puppy will stop whining.

— MIKE DITKA,
former NFL coach and Hall of Fame tight end,
from *Webster's Electronic Quotebase*, edited by Keith Mohler,
1994

If you're associated with the Philadelphia media or town, you look for negatives . . . I don't know if there's something in the air or something about their upbringing or they have too many hoagies, too much cream cheese.

— MIKE SCHMIDT,
Hall of Fame third baseman for the Philadelphia Phillies,
referring to the Philadelphia media,
as quoted in *USA Today*, March 9, 1989

Some media people are preoccupied with taunting, badmouthing and emphasizing mistakes and slip-ups instead of achievements. I wish they'd pay—and educate fans to pay—more respectful attention to the strains these young kids endure in a hard-fought game. I wish sports reporters wouldn't try to make themselves look good by putting words into the mouths of stressed and inexperienced 19-year-olds, leading them to say something about their teammates, or their opponents, or their coach, so that the reporter can get a headline and byline by making a kid look bad.

— JOE PATERNO,
longtime head football coach at Penn State,
from his book *Paterno: By the Book*, with Bernard Asbell,
1989

The Meaning of Life

When I was going through my transition of being famous, I tried to ask God why was I here. What was my purpose? Surely, it wasn't just to win three gold medals. There has to be more to this life than that.

—WILMA RUDOLPH,
   U.S. track athlete and winner of three gold medals in the
      1960 Olympics,
   in *I Dream a World* by Brian Lanker, 1989

Memories

No, I don't have any regrets. Not about one damned thing. I've had a lot of good experiences in my life, and they far outnumber the bad. Good memories are the greatest thing in the world, and I've got a lot of those. And one of the sweetest is of the kid standing out on the green grass in center field, with the winning runs on base, saying to himself, "Hit it to me. Hit it to me."

—PETE REISER,
   former major league outfielder,
   as quoted in the *50th Anniversary Hall of Fame Yearbook*,
      1989

A man who has put away his baseball togs after an eventful life in the game must live on his memories, some good, some bad.

—BABE RUTH,
   legendary Hall of Fame outfielder,
   from *The Babe Ruth Story* by Babe Ruth, as told to
      Bob Consadine, 1948

 *Mental Aptitude*

The good Lord was good to me. He gave me a strong body, a good right arm, and a weak mind.

— DIZZY DEAN,
baseball pitcher and broadcaster,
as quoted in *Grand Slams and Fumbles* by Peter Beilenson

I could have been a Rhodes Scholar, except for my grades.

— DUFFY DAUGHERTY,
head football coach at Michigan State,
as quoted in the *The Book of Football Wisdom*, edited by
Criswell Freeman, 1996

I owe everything to golf. Where else could a guy with an IQ like mine make this much money?

— HUBERT GREEN,
professional golfer,
as quoted in *Golfers on Golf*, edited by Downs MacRury, 1997

If you can say the morale of your club is good after losing 10 out of 12 games, then your intelligence is a little low.

— PAUL RICHARDS,
while he was manager of the Baltimore Orioles,
as quoted in *Baseball's Greatest Quotations* by Paul Dickson,
1991

I'm going to Radio Shack to buy one of those headsets like the broadcasters use. It seems as soon as you put them on, you get 100 times smarter.

— NICK LEYVA,
former Philadelphia Phillies manager,
tired of criticism from the TV booth,
as quoted in the *Boston Herald*, July 29, 1990

Nobody in football should be called a genius. A genius is a guy like Norman Einstein.

>   ✎ JOE THEISMANN,
>   football commentator and former quarterback for the Washington Redskins,
>   as quoted on *Success For You.net*

The dumber a pitcher is, the better. When he gets smart and begins to experiment with a lot of different pitches, he's in trouble. All I ever had was a fastball, a curve, and a changeup. And I did pretty good.

>   ✎ DIZZY DEAN,
>   baseball pitcher and broadcaster,
>   as quoted in *Baseball Digest*, August 1961

Why would anyone expect him to come out smarter? He went to prison for four years, not Princeton.

>   ✎ DAN DUVA,
>   boxing promoter,
>   referring to boxer Mike Tyson's decision to hook up again
>   with promoter Don King,
>   as quoted on *Success For You.net*

I ain't afraid to tell the world that it don't take school stuff to help a fella play ball.

>   ✎ "SHOELESS" JOE JACKSON,
>   Negro League superstar who was illiterate,
>   widely attributed

It really helps to be stupid if you're a relief pitcher. You can't be thinking about too many things. You can't be on the mound worrying about a 35-inning streak where you haven't given up a double to a left-handed batter or something. Relief pitchers have to get into a zone of their own. I just hope I'm stupid enough.

>   ✎ DAN QUISENBERRY,
>   former major league relief pitcher,
>   as quoted in the *Los Angeles Times*, June 26, 1982

The Mind

Your mind is what makes everything else work.

—KAREEM ABDUL-JABBAR,
Hall of Fame basketball player,
in *The Ultimate Success Quotations Library*, Cyber Nation
International, Inc., Reno, NV, 1997

The mind is the limit. As long as the mind can envision the fact that you can do something, you can do it—as long as you really believe 100 percent.

—ARNOLD SCHWARZENEGGER,
bodybuilder and actor,
as quoted in *Get Lost Adventure Magazine*

I can do something else besides stuff a ball through a hoop. My biggest resource is my mind.

—KAREEM ABDUL-JABBAR,
Hall of Fame basketball player,
in *The Ultimate Success Quotations Library*, Cyber Nation
International, Inc., Reno, NV, 1997

Misfortune

Look at misfortune the same way you look at success: Don't panic. Do your best and forget the consequences.

—WALTER ALSTON,
former manager of the Los Angeles Dodgers,
widely known as his playing credo

Mistakes

I'm not allowed to make mistakes. You make a mistake and it's magnified. It makes you scared to live your life.

> ━MICHAEL JORDAN,
> former NBA superstar with the Chicago Bulls,
> after allegations that he had a serious gambling problem

It stays with me to this day. It's like I ran over a deer in my car. I won't forget it.

> ━SCOTTIE PIPPEN,
> professional basketball player and named one of the 50 greatest
> players in NBA history,
> referring to his refusal to play the last 1.8 seconds of an
> Eastern Conference semifinal game between the Chicago
> Bulls and the New York Knicks because of a disagreement
> he had with his then-coach, Phil Jackson

No regrets, not a single one. Maybe the only thing I'm truly sorry about is hitting one guy in the face with a pitch. It was Jimmie Hall and he was with Minnesota and it was a damn accident. He was never the same again. A thing like that stays with you. I almost cost a guy his life.

> ━BO BELINSKY,
> professional baseball pitcher,
> reflecting on 15 years in the sport,
> as quoted in *Bo: Pitching and Wooing*

I think if I had my life to live over again, I would do things a little different. I was aggressive, perhaps too aggressive, maybe I went too far. I always had to be right in any argument I was in, and wanted to be first in everything.

> ━TY COBB,
> legendary major league baseball player, manager and Hall of
> Famer,
> as quoted in *Baseball As I Have Known It* by Fred G. Lieb, 1976

Your Honor, I would like to say that I am very sorry. I am very shameful to be here today in front of you. I think I'm perceived as a very aggressive, arrogant type of individual. But I want people to know that I do have emotion, I do have feelings, and I can be hurt like everybody else. And I hope that no one has to go through what I went through the last year and a half. I lost my dignity, I lost my self-respect, I lost a lot of dear fans and almost lost some very dear friends.

—PETE ROSE,
former major league player and the all-time leader in hits,
to Judge Arthur Spiegel when Rose was being sentenced on
July 19, 1990 for tax evasion

Looking back, I think I handled that wrong. Instead of popping off in front of the team that I felt he had offended, I wish I had held my peace, met Franco privately later, and tried to dig out what was bugging him.

—JOE PATERNO,
longtime Penn State football coach,
referring to the time in 1971 when he exploded at then-Penn
State player Franco Harris for being late for a practice,
from his book *Paterno: By the Book*, with Bernard Asbell, 1989

I'm a little too belligerent. I cuss and swear at people. I yell at umpires and maybe I'm a little too tough at home sometimes. I don't sign as many autographs as I should and I haven't always been very good with the writers.

—THURMAN MUNSON,
former catcher for the New York Yankees, who was killed in a
plane crash in 1979;
this quote served as his epitaph, appearing in several versions
of his obituary

I regret to this day that I never went to college. I feel I should have been a doctor.

—TY COBB,
legendary major league baseball player, manager and Hall of
Famer,
widely quoted

Money

When you're fighting, you're fighting for one thing—money.

➤ JACK DEMPSEY,
  former world heavyweight champion,
  as quoted in *The Guinness Dictionary of Sports Quotations*
      by Colin Jarman, 1990

You can ask your kid, "Do you want to go to the Skydome or Europe?"

➤ PAT SHERIDAN,
  former major league outfielder,
  referring to the $6.50 hot dogs and $3.50 beers at the new
      Skydome in Toronto,
  as quoted in the *Dallas Morning News*, June 18, 1989

Tell you what, you keep the salary and pay me the cut.

➤ LEFTY GOMEZ,
  Hall of Fame pitcher for the New York Yankees during the
      1930s,
  when asked to take a cut in salary from $20,000 to $7,500
      following a poor season,
  as quoted in *The Guinness Dictionary of Sports Quotations*
      by Colin Jarman, 1990

Ninety percent I'll spend on good times, women and Irish whiskey. The other 10 percent I'll probably waste.

➤ TUG MCGRAW,
  former relief pitcher for the New York Mets and Philadelphia
      Phillies,
  referring to how he planned to spend his 1975 salary of
      $75,000

If you're paid before you walk on the court, what's the point in playing as if your life depended on it?

➤ ARTHUR ASHE,
  Hall of Fame tennis player and AIDS activist,
  from *The Speaker's Electronic Reference Collection*, AApex
      Software, 1994

It's just getting crazy. Shocked? Yes. How can you pay a ballplayer $3 million or $3.5 million a year when the head of the Chiefs of Staffs is making just $77,000 a year? Some way, somehow, someone has to say "Stop!" Can one man make a $3 million difference in a ballclub? I don't know.

➤ GEORGE STEINBRENNER,
   controversial owner of the New York Yankees,
   as quoted in the *Washington Times*, January 29, 1990

A man ought to get all he can earn. A man who knows he's making money for other people ought to get some of the profit he brings in. Don't make any difference if it's baseball or a bank or a vaudeville show. It's business, I tell you. There ain't no sentiment to it. Forget that stuff.

➤ BABE RUTH,
   legendary Hall of Fame outfielder,
   as quoted in *Babe: The Legend Comes to Life* by Robert W.
   Creamer, 1974

I'm not easily fooled. I may come out on the short end of the stick, but it's not because I didn't know any better. For example, I've loaned money to people—in some cases quite a bit of money. Then someone says to me, "Gee, I need five hundred or a thousand dollars and I'll pay you back," chances are I won't get the money back. It's happened several times, even with friends . . . As far as I'm concerned, once I give money, I figure I'll never see it again. If I do, I'm pleasantly surprised.

➤ ARTHUR ASHE,
   Hall of Fame tennis player and AIDS activist,
   in his book *Off the Court*, with Neil Admur

Man, if I made a million dollars, I would come in at six in the morning, sweep the stands, wash the uniforms, clean out the offices, manage the team and play the games.

➤ DUKE SNIDER,
   Hall of Fame outfielder, turned broadcaster,
   referring to players' salaries,
   as quoted in *Sport*, April 1980

It's not if you look at it from the standpoint of the national debt.

> ➤BILL RIGNEY,
> former manager of the Minnesota Twins,
> when asked if the team's earned run average was astronomical,
> as quoted in *The Sporting News*, April 25, 1970

Players are funny. They respect guys who make a lot of money, even if they don't deserve it. The manager is the most important guy on the team and should be treated on a higher level. Coaches should be regarded highly, too, but because of their comparatively low salaries, they're not. I don't think that's fair.

> ➤JOE MORGAN,
> Hall of Fame second baseman, turned broadcaster,
> as quoted in *Sports Illustrated*, April 16, 1983

I am broke financially but full of ambition. It is like starting all over again for me and I love baseball and I love to build up teams. I have done it once and will do it again.

> ➤CONNIE MACK,
> legendary manager of the Philadelphia Athletics,
> looking at his future in 1915,
> as quoted in *Baseball: An Informal History* by Douglass
>   Wallop

I feel we're all overpaid. Every professional athlete is overpaid. I got a phenomenal contract—much more money than I ever thought I'd make. I wouldn't say I'm embarrassed by it, but deep down I know I'm not worth it. To my shame, though, I have to admit I asked for it.

> ➤FRED PATEK,
> former shortstop for the Kansas City Royals,
> as quoted in *Late Innings* by Roger Angell, 1982

We traveled four in a berth and when it came to meal times, the manager would put down a silver dollar for the whole team.

> ➤CONNIE MACK,
> legendary manager of the Philadelphia Athletics,
> referring to his first trip to spring training as a player,
> as quoted in *The Sporting News*, April 20, 1955

Beer makes some players happy. Winning ballgames makes some players happy. Cashing checks makes me delirious with joy.

> ►JIM BROSNAN,
> professional baseball player,
> as quoted in *Sport*, December 1963

The rules are changed now. There's not any way to build a team today. It's just how much money you want to spend. You could be the world champions, and somebody else makes a key acquisition or two and you're through.

> ►WHITEY HERZOG,
> former major league manager,
> talking about the state of the game during the time he was
>   managing the Kansas City Royals

I'm working as hard as I can to get my life and my cash to run out at the same time. If I can just die after lunch Tuesday, everything will be perfect.

> ►DOUG SANDERS,
> professional golfer,
> as quoted in *Golfers on Golf*, edited by Downs MacRury, 1997

When you're President, do something about taxes. They're killing me.

> ►BILLY LOES,
> professional baseball player,
> on meeting Vice President Richard Nixon,
> as quoted in *Sport*, August 1960

I figured I'd better sign before I owed them money.

> ►JERRY KOOSMAN,
> former major league pitcher,
> on signing with the Mets for $1200 when the original offer
>   had been $1600, then lowered several times

Guarantee me $3 million a year and you can scream, yell or spit on my ball when I'm putting. Because even if I miss it, I still get paid.

> ►LEE TREVINO,
> Hall of Fame golfer,
> referring to the guaranteed contracts of baseball and football
>   players

We live in a materialistic society in which money doesn't only talk—it screams. I could not forget that some of the very ballplayers who swore the most fervently that they wouldn't play with me because I was black were the first to begin helping me, giving me tips and advice, as soon as they became aware that I could be helpful to them in winning the few thousand more dollars players receive as World Series champs. The most prejudiced of the club owners were not as upset about the game being contaminated by blacks as they were fearing that integration would hurt them in their pocketbooks.

➤ JACKIE ROBINSON,
    first African-American baseball player to play in the major
      leagues,
    in *I Never Had It Made: An Autobiography* by Jackie Robinson,
      as told to Alfred Duckett, 1972

Jimmy Connors plays two tennis matches and winds up with $850,000, and Muhammad Ali fights one bout and winds up with five million bucks. Me, I play 190 games—if you count exhibitions—and *I'm* overpaid!

➤ JOHNNY BENCH,
    Hall of Fame catcher for the Cincinnati Reds,
    referring to his $175,000 salary,
    as quoted in the *New York Times*, May 25, 1975

I don't like money, actually, but it quiets my nerves.

➤ JOE LOUIS,
    former world heavyweight champion,
    as quoted in *The Guinness Dictionary of Sports Quotations*
      by Colin Jarman, 1990

Because we dress very well on the course, people think we're all millionaires. The truth is that there is less money in pro golf than in any well-known sport. Out of the 144 guys here, at least 100 are extremely concerned about their next check.

➤ ED SNEED,
    professional golfer,
    as quoted in *Golfers on Golf*, edited by Downs MacRury,
      1997

My wife always said she wanted to marry a millionaire. Well, she married a millionaire. I used to be a multimillionaire.

—LEE TREVINO,
Hall of Fame golfer,
as quoted in *Golfers on Golf*, edited by Downs MacRury, 1997

She knows how to hang onto her money. I wish her mom were the same way.

—ORVILLE MOODY,
professional golfer,
referring to his daughter/caddie,
as quoted in *Golfers on Golf*, edited by Downs MacRury, 1997

There's so much money to be made today in Monday events and at foreign tournaments that it's hard for anyone to dominate. It's a lot harder to concentrate on big events when you have so many lucrative distractions.

—JACK NICKLAUS,
Hall of Fame golfer and winner of 20 major championships,
as quoted in *Golfers on Golf*, edited by Downs MacRury, 1997

I like the idea of playing for money instead of silverware. I never did like to polish.

—PATTY SHEEHAN,
Hall of Fame golfer,
as quoted in *Golfers on Golf*, edited by Downs MacRury, 1997

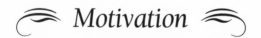

Motivation

Getting hit motivates me. It makes me punish the guy more. A fighter takes a punch, hits back with three punches.

—ROBERTO DURAN,
former world welterweight champion,
as quoted in *Newsweek*, June 23, 1980, prior to Duran
defeating Sugar Ray Leonard for the championship

When we were in Toronto earlier in the year, someone wrote I wouldn't be in the top 10. When I read something like that, it gives me the drive to do what they say I can't do.

    ➤WAYNE GRETZKY,
      hockey superstar,
      referring to an article that appeared during his first year as a
        professional player,
      as quoted in *The Great One: The Life and Times of Wayne
        Gretzky* by Andrew Podnieks, 1999

I motivate players through communication, being honest with them, having them respect and appreciate your ability and your help. I started in the minor leagues. I used to hug my players when they did something well. That's my enthusiasm. That's my personality. I jump with joy when we win. I try to be on a close basis with my players. People say you can't go out to eat with your players. I say, why not?

    ➤TOMMY LASORDA,
      former manager of the Los Angeles Dodgers,
      as quoted in the *New York Times*, May 17, 1982

I am not an animal in my personal life. But in the ring there is an animal inside me. Sometimes it roars when the first bell rings. Sometimes it springs out later in a fight. But I can always feel it there, driving me and pushing me forward. It is what makes me win. It makes me enjoy fighting.

    ➤ROBERTO DURAN,
      former world welterweight champion,
      as quoted in *Newsweek*, June 23, 1980, prior to Duran
        defeating Sugar Ray Leonard for the championship

Music

Music washes away from the soul the dust of everyday life.

➤ RED AUERBACH,
    legendary Hall of Fame basketball coach who led the Boston
        Celtics to nine NBA championships,
    as quoted in the *Speaker's Electronic Reference Collection*,
        AApex Software, 1994

Obstacles

I had a series of childhood illnesses . . . scarlet fever . . . pneumonia . . . polio. I walked with braces until I was at least 9 years old.
My life wasn't like the average person who grew up and decided to
enter the world of sports.

➤ WILMA RUDOLPH,
    U.S. track athlete and winner of three gold medals in the
        1960 Olympics,
    as quoted in *USA Today*, August 6, 1987

If I wasn't dyslexic, I probably wouldn't have won the Games. If I
had been a better reader, then that would have come easily, sports
would have come easily . . . and I never would have realized that
the way you get ahead in life is hard work.

➤ BRUCE JENNER,
    1976 Olympic gold medalist in the decathlon and later a
        sportscaster,
    as quoted in the *Los Angeles Times*, June 23, 1996

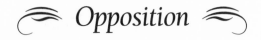

Opposition

But I've never lost a street fight . . . to a woman.

⌐TENNIELLE SMITH,
    a hairdresser and aspiring professional woman boxer,
        scheduled to fight Jacqueline "Sister Smoke" Frazier-Lyde,
        daughter of boxer Joe Frazier

Optimism

The guys seem real positive. Evidently, they're not reading the papers.

⌐MIKE DITKA,
    former New Orleans Saints coach,
    after a good practice

Optimism is a tremendously important ingredient anywhere along the way, but especially the older you get.

⌐JIM LAW,
    a sprinter from Charlotte, North Carolina, who at age 65
        broke the record for the 400-meter dash in the 65 to 69 age
        bracket,
    as quoted in *December Champions* by Rob Darden and W.R.
        Spence, M.D., 1993

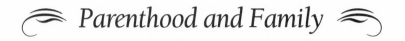

Parenthood and Family

The great high of winning Wimbledon lasts for about a week. You go down in the record book, but you don't have anything tangible to hold on to. But having a baby—there isn't any comparison.

━CHRIS EVERT,
   Hall of Fame tennis player and three-time Wimbledon
      champion,
   in *The Last Word: A Treasury of Women's Quotes* by Carolyn
      Warner, 1992

You cross first base over to third and home plate over to second.

━JIMMY PIERSALL,
   major league outfielder and father of 10,
   explaining how to pin diapers,
   as quoted in *Sportswit* by Lee Green, 1984

I called the doctor and he told me the contraptions were an hour apart.

━MACKEY SASSER,
   former major league baseball player,
   telling how he knew his wife was in labor in 1988 when
      Sasser was a catcher for the New York Mets

I have so much fun being at home, getting up in the morning, making breakfast, taking my kids to school, going to school activities. That's where my life is right now.

━PAYNE STEWART,
   professional golfer and two-time U.S. Open champion,
   shortly before his death in a plane crash in October, 1999

Some children never have their fathers for any years, and I had mine for almost 31. No one can convince me that I was unlucky.

━MICHAEL JORDAN,
   former NBA superstar with the Chicago Bulls,
   after his father, James Jordan, was robbed and murdered in
      1993

As a father, I just want to be there for my kids. To help them learn, to help them enjoy life and yet, give them discipline, guidance.

➤ MICHAEL JORDAN,
  former NBA superstar with the Chicago Bulls and father of
    three children,
  as quoted in *Ebony* magazine, November 1991

Football was the furthest thing from my mind. My grandmother basically raised me and has always been my inspiration and my source of strength. There were so many things I wanted to say to her, and I prayed that I would be able to see her again.

➤ DEONTEY KENNER,
  quarterback for the University of Cincinnati,
  who was told after his team's upset win over Wisconsin on
    September 18, 1999, that his grandmother had suffered
    heart failure and would be undergoing emergency surgery,
  as quoted in *Sports Illustrated*, October 11, 1999

My mother was watching on television and she doesn't want me to hurt anyone.

➤ GEORGE FOREMAN,
  Olympic gold medalist and former heavyweight champion of
    the world,
  on why he didn't knock out his opponent during the 1968
    Olympics

My dream is to be able to pay back my mother and grandmother for all the sacrifices they've made for me. If I can do that with the NFL, that's great, but if I can't, I want to make sure I can take care of them through my work. It might take me a little longer, but I'll do it.

➤ DEONTEY KENNER,
  quarterback for the University of Cincinnati,
  referring to his determination to earn a degree in exercise
    physiology,
  as quoted in *Sports Illustrated*, October 11, 1999

My sister's expecting a baby, and I don't know if I'm going to be an uncle or an aunt.

    ━CHUCK NEVITT,
        North Carolina State basketball player,
        explaining to Coach Jim Valvano why he appeared nervous at
           practice

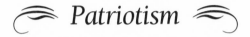

Patriotism

I do this for myself because I am my own fatherland, and my handkerchief is my flag.

    ━REINHOLD MESSNER,
        mountain climber, after climbing the 14 highest mountains in
           the world,
        as quoted in *Time*, October 27, 1986

Waving the flag at the 1976 Olympics wasn't my idea. It was too much apple pie and ice cream. Not that I don't love my country, but I felt it was my victory up there, I put all the time into it.

    ━BRUCE JENNER,
        1976 Olympic gold medalist in the decathlon and later a
           sportscaster,
        from a CBS *SportsLine* interview, July1980

People

Nice guys. Finish last.

    ━LEO DUROCHER,
        former manager of the Brooklyn Dodgers and New York
           Giants,
        a casual remark at a practice ground in July 1946.
        Generally quoted as "Nice guys finish last."

Perseverance

If you run into a wall, don't turn around and give up. Figure out how to climb it, go through it, or work around it.

> ━MICHAEL JORDAN,
> former NBA superstar with the Chicago Bulls,
> in *I Can't Accept Not Trying: Michael Jordan on the Pursuit of Excellence*, 1994

There were lots of times when I could have won but didn't. But I persevered and eventually I learned that you don't have to hit the ball perfectly to win; you have to manage yourself better.

> ━TOM WATSON,
> Hall of Fame golfer,
> as quoted in *Golfers on Golf*, edited by Downs MacRury, 1997

Just keep going. Everybody gets better if they keep at it.

> ━TED WILLIAMS,
> legendary Hall of Fame outfielder with the Boston Red Sox,
> from *The Speaker's Electronic Reference Collection*, AApex Software, 1994

We fight until they take the last breath out of us.

> ━DARRYL TALLEY,
> former Buffalo Bills linebacker,
> after the Bills came back from 35-3 to beat the Houston Oilers in a 1992 American Football Conference playoff game

I don't feel sorry for myself, because that's the first step of giving up, and I'm not giving up. I know something good is going to come of this. I just haven't figured out what it is yet.

> ━WALTER PAYTON,
> Hall of Fame running back for the Chicago Bears,
> in an interview with *Sports Illustrated* writer Don Yaeger, shortly before Payton's death from liver disease and cancer in November 1999

 *Perspective*

Don 't hurry. Don't worry. You're only here for a short visit. So don't forget to stop and smell the roses.

➤ WALTER HAGEN,
Hall of Fame golfer, widely credited for raising the social standing of professional golfing,
as quoted in *The Golfer's Book of Wisdom*, edited by Criswell Freeman, 1995

Sometimes it takes years to really grasp what has happened to your life.

➤ WILMA RUDOLPH,
U.S. track athlete and winner of three gold medals in the 1960 Olympics,
in *Words of Women: Quotations for Success* by Power Dynamics Publishing, 1997

Life consists of a lot of minor annoyances and a few matters of real consequence.

➤ HARVEY PENICK,
legendary golf instructor,
as quoted in *The Golfer's Book of Wisdom*, edited by Criswell Freeman, 1995

Twenty years from now, I can look at this medal and say, "I was the best quarter-miler in the world on that day." If you don't think that's important, you don't know what's inside an athlete's soul.

➤ VINCE MATTHEWS,
U.S. 1972 Olympic gold medalist,
as quoted in news summaries, December 31, 1972

Fifty years from now I'll be just three inches of type in a record book.

➤ BROOKS ROBINSON,
Baltimore Orioles Hall of Fame third baseman,
as quoted in *Sport*, October 1963

Each time I visit a children's hospital I get a reality check. I realize that missing a jump or having a bad practice isn't the end of the world. I'm reminded of how lucky I've been.

➤ TARA LIPINSKI,
   Olympic gold medalist and world figure skating champion,
   in her autobiography, *Tara* Lipinski: *Triumph on Ice,* with
      Emily Costello, 1998

We are reminded how short life really is, and how we are just passing through. So, all the people you haven't told you love lately, tell them, and live your days like you mean it.

➤ HAL SUTTON,
   professional golfer,
   reflecting on life after the death of fellow golfer Payne Stewart
      in October 1999

I felt like, wow, what a great way to make a living. If I goof up, there's going to be a relief pitcher come in there. Nobody's going to shoot me.

➤ WARREN SPAHN,
   Hall of Fame pitcher with the Milwaukee Braves,
   on returning to the game after serving in World War II,
   as quoted in *USA Today*, May 25, 1990

When you 're playing for the national championship, it's not a matter of life and death. It's more important than that.

➤ DUFFY DAUGHERTY,
   head football coach at Michigan State University from 1954 to
      1972, winner of the national title in 1965,
   as quoted in the *The Book of Football Wisdom*, edited by
      Criswell Freeman, 1996

When somebody on your team does that, you say: "What guts. What a gamer." When a guy on the other team does it, you say: "What a dummy. There's no percentage in that." When it's the other guy, you become a cynic.

➤ RAY MILLER,
   former pitching coach for the Baltimore Orioles,
   referring to a player hitting the wall in order to make a catch

There's something else to live for, something else to come home to. I've got a wife, a son and a daughter and they are so much more important to me than golf.

— NICK PRICE,
professional golfer,
as quoted in *Golfers on Golf*, edited by Downs MacRury, 1997

Oh, until about five minutes after I'm dead.

— BILL SHEA,
a New York Mets executive,
when asked how long he thought Shea Stadium would remain
with that name,
as quoted in *Joy in Mudville* by George Vecsey, 1970

If you react the same way to winning and losing, that's a big accomplishment. That quality is important because it stays with you the rest of your life, and there's going to be a life after tennis that's a lot longer than your tennis life.

— CHRIS EVERT,
Hall of Fame tennis player,
in *Good Advice* by William Safire and Leonard Safire, 1982

The man who views the world at 50 the same as he did at 20 has wasted 30 years of his life.

— MUHAMMAD ALI,
Olympic gold medalist and former world heavyweight champion,
as quoted in *Playboy,* November 1975

Pessimism

Slim and none. And slim just went out the door.

— SCOTTIE PIPPEN,
named one of the 50 greatest players in NBA history and
former member of the world champion Chicago Bulls,
speaking in January 2000 on the Bulls' chances of regaining
championship form quickly

Practice

Practice, which some regard as a chore, should be approached as just about the most pleasant recreation ever devised.

➤BABE DIDRIKSON ZAHARIAS,
    Hall of Fame golfer, and Olympic champion,
    as quoted in *The Golfer's Book of Wisdom*, edited by Criswell
        Freeman, 1995

It's not necessarily the amount of time you spend at practice that counts; it's what you put into the practice.

➤ERIC LINDROS,
    Philadelphia Flyers center,
    as quoted in *Get Lost Adventure Magazine*

Undirected practice is worse than no practice. Too often you become careless and sloppy in your swing. You'd be better off staying home and beating the rugs.

➤GARY PLAYER,
    Hall of Fame golfer,
    as quoted in *Golfers on Golf*, edited by Downs MacRury, 1997

Practice sometimes leads to fiddling and experimenting—and that can be damaging.

➤IAN WOOSNAM,
    professional golfer,
    as quoted in *Golfers on Golf*, edited by Downs MacRury, 1997

It's good to practice (golf) at night. You hit the ball and listen. If you hear crack-crack-crack, you know you have hit the trees. Lost ball. But you hear nothing, you know you are in the middle of the fairway.

➤COSTANTINO ROCCA,
    professional golfer,
    as quoted in *Golfers on Golf*, edited by Downs MacRury, 1997

Practice until you don't have to think.

◄─CALVIN PEETE,
professional golfer,
as quoted in *Golfers on Golf*, edited by Downs MacRury, 1997

The harder I practice, the luckier I get.

◄─GARY PLAYER,
Hall of Fame golfer,
as quoted in *Golfers on Golf*, edited by Downs MacRury, 1997

Life doesn't give you all the practice races you need.

◄─JESSE OWENS,
the greatest sprinter of his generation, winner of four gold
medals at the Berlin Olympics in 1936,
from an Internet collection of quotations

 *Pressure*

We all choke. You just try to choke last.

◄─TOM WATSON,
Hall of Fame golfer,
as quoted in *Golfers on Golf*, edited by Downs MacRury, 1997

Putting affects the nerves more than anything else. I would actually
get nauseated over three-footers, and there were tournaments
when I couldn't get a meal down for four days.

◄─BYRON NELSON,
Hall of Fame golfer, who won 11 consecutive tournaments in
1945,
as quoted in *Golfers on Golf*, edited by Downs MacRury, 1997

Pressure is playing for $10 when you don't have a dime in your
pocket.

◄─LEE TREVINO,
Hall of Fame golfer,
as quoted in *Golfers on Golf*, edited by Downs MacRury, 1997

The pressure gets worse the older you get. The hole starts to look the size of a Bayer aspirin.

> ━GARY PLAYER,
> Hall of Fame golfer,
> as quoted in *Golfers on Golf*, edited by Downs MacRury,
> 1997

 *Pride*

Great champions have an enormous sense of pride. The people who excel are those who are driven to show the world and prove to themselves just how good they are.

> ━NANCY LOPEZ,
> Hall of Fame golfer,
> as quoted in *The Golfer's Book of Wisdom*, edited by Criswell
> Freeman, 1995

What I miss when I'm away is the pride in baseball. Especially the pride of being on a team that wins. I probably was the proudest Yankee of them all. And I don't mean false pride. When it's real on a team, it's a deep love pride. There's nothing greater in the world than when somebody on the team does something good, and everybody gathers around to pat him on the back. I really love the togetherness in baseball. That's a real true love.

> ━BILLY MARTIN,
> former New York Yankees player and manager,
> as quoted in *Sports Illustrated*, June 2, 1975

Publicity

Publicity is like poison; it doesn't hurt unless you swallow it.

—JOE PATERNO,
  longtime head football coach at Penn State,
  from *The Speaker's Electronic Reference Collection*, AApex
    Software, 1994

I think I have gotten more publicity for doing less than any player
who ever lived.

—BO BELINSKY,
  professional baseball pitcher,
  as quoted in *Catcher in the Wry*, Bob Uecker with Mickey
    Herskowitz, 1981

Having a low profile helps keep everything in perspective. In January I got my hair cut a couple of days after winning the Phoenix
Open by 12 shots. A woman in the salon told me all about the tournament, how her boyfriend had brought her tickets and how she
saw Tiger (Woods) make a hole in one. I said, "Oh really? Who
won the tournament?" She said, "Hmmm, I'm not sure." "Thanks
a lot," I thought, though I never told her who I was.

—STEVE JONES,
  professional golfer,
  talking about how he's rarely recognized by the public,
  as quoted in *Sports Illustrated*, July 21, 1997

Believe me, publicity isn't what it's made out to be.

—PETE ROSE,
  former major league baseball player and the all-time leader in
    hits,
  to his teammate Kal Daniels, who, when Daniels was traded
    by the Cincinnati Reds to the Los Angeles Dodgers,
    complained that he'd received very little publicity,
  as quoted in *Sports Illustrated*, July 31, 1989

It's just hard for me to go anywhere not unnoticed—in the sense of getting out in the public and trying to enjoy myself without people bothering me. This was the last area that I could go to where no one really knew who I was to some degree. And now it's been exposed.

> ✦ MICHAEL JORDAN,
> former NBA superstar with the Chicago Bulls,
> recalling when he could visit Paris without being mobbed by
> fans,
> as quoted by the Associated Press on cbs.sportsline.com, 1998

I have had a few bits of publicity. I don't find publicity annoying or anything, I just take it for what it's worth. People who are interested in pursuing that type of activity, that's fine. I don't resist, but I don't over-emphasize it, either. I feel I'm just plain lucky, so I'm not going to trade on it. I take publicity very lightly.

> ✦ KEN BEER,
> a Hillsborough, California tennis player, who, since starting
> to play competitively at age 60 has won more than 70
> national tournaments,
> as quoted in *December Champions* by Bob Darden and W.R.
> Spence, M.D., 1993

I want to walk down the street and hear them say, "Jesus, there goes Dick Stuart!" I crave publicity.

> ✦ DICK STUART,
> former first baseman the Boston Red Sox,
> as quoted in *Sport*, December 1963

I never wanted all this hoopla. All I wanted is to be a good ballplayer, hit 25 or 30 homers, drive in around a hundred runs, hit .280 and help my club win pennants. I just wanted to be one of the guys, an average player having an average season.

> ✦ ROGER MARIS,
> former New York Yankees right fielder,
> after hitting his record-breaking, 61st home run during the
> 1961 season,
> as quoted in *My Greatest Days in Baseball* by Jack Orr, 1996

I don't read many truths in the paper. Then again, I haven't read the papers. But I hear about it. It would scare me to read the paper. I didn't know I had enough time to do the things I'm supposed to be doing. I'm tired of seeing my picture on the front page of *USA Today*. That's the only paper I get. But you can't put much stock in papers. They only cost 50 cents.

> ➤ PETE ROSE,
>> former major league baseball player and the all-time leader in hits,
>> responding to allegations about his gambling,
>> as quoted in *The Sporting News*, July 17, 1989

It's a weird scene. You win a few baseball games and all of a sudden you're surrounded by reporters and TV men with cameras asking you about Vietnam and race relations.

> ➤ VIDA BLUE,
>> former major league pitcher,
>> as quoted in the *Los Angeles Times*, April 14, 1982

I'm tired of seeing my name in big print. I don't like being a bumper sticker. You know, "If You Drink, Don't Drive," that kind of stuff: "Vida Blue is Beautiful!"

> ➤ VIDA BLUE,
>> former major league pitcher,
>> from *Vida: His Own Story* by Bill Libby and Vida Blue, 1972

Baseball's a routine. You're doing the same thing day in, day out. You try to reach a certain level and once you're there you try to maintain it. If you don't do it one day there's always the next, and it always comes in a hurry. You can be headlines as a hero one day, and a goat the next.

> ➤ GREG LUZINSKI,
>> former major league baseball player,
>> as quoted in the *Chicago Tribune*, May 2, 1982

Quitting

All quitters are good losers.

> —BOB ZUPPKE,
> former college football coach, who is credited with introduc-
> ing the offensive huddle in the early 1920s,
> as quoted in *The Book of Football Wisdom*, edited by Criswell
> Freeman, 1996

If you want to get off this team, you have to take a number.

> —DAVE REVERING,
> former New York Yankee,
> said just before he was traded to the Toronto Blue Jays in
> 1981,
> as quoted in *The Official New York Yankee Hater's Handbook*
> by William B. Mead

Dear Son:

Received your letter and am sorry to hear that you are so homesick. You will notice that I did not forward any money for your passage to Philadelphia. The reason was not that I didn't have it to send to you, but that you were trying to tell me in your letter that you wanted to come home right away. Edward, I have tears in my eyes while I'm telling you this, but if you do come home, please do not come to 915 East Russell Street. We do not want quitters in this family.

Your Mother.

> —MOTHER OF EDDIE STANKY, former major league player and
> manager,
> responding to a letter in which her son, shortly after breaking
> into baseball, wrote and asked for money to come home
> because he was homesick,
> as quoted in *The Sporting News* in 1951

Racism

Apartheid is handled with such sophistication that it is sometimes easy to forget that South Africa is nothing less than a police state.

— ARTHUR ASHE,
    Hall of Fame tennis player and AIDS activist,
    in his book *Portrait in Motion*, with Frank Deford, 1975

Shaking hands with the Queen of England was a long way from being forced to sit in the colored section of the bus going into downtown Wilmington, North Carolina.

— ALTHEA GIBSON,
    Hall of Fame tennis player and the first African-American to
        win the U.S. Open and Wimbledon championships,
    on being the first African-American to win at Wimbledon,
    in *Women-Sports* magazine, March 1976

As far as I'm concerned, the signing of Satchel Paige to a Cleveland contract is far more interesting than was the news when Branch Rickey broke the baseball color line by signing Jackie Robinson to a Montreal contract. It was inevitable that the bigotry which kept Negroes out of organized ball would be beaten back, but I'd never heard of Robinson at that time. With Paige it's different. The Satchmo has been a baseball legend for a long time, a Paul Bunyan in technicolor. More fabulous tales have been told of Satchel's pitching ability than of any pitcher in organized baseball.

— TOM MEANY,
    as quoted in *Maybe I'll Pitch Forever* by Satchel Paige, as told
        to David Lipman, 1962

On the field, blacks have been able to be super giants. But once our playing days are over, this is the end of it and we go back to the back of the bus again.

— HANK AARON,
    Hall of Fame outfielder and the all-time home run leader,
    as quoted in *Hammerin' Hank: The Henry Aaron Story*, by Dan
        Schlossberg, 1974

Let's face it, there are folks down here who just don't want their kids growing up to admire a Negro ballplayer, even if he's Willie Mays or Hank Aaron.

    ➤SAM SMITH,
       president of the Southern League,
       as quoted in *America through Baseball* by David Q. Voigt, 1976

It was the day of integration at a school. The mobs were outside, screaming, cursing, carrying signs. A Negro woman came through the mob with her little girl and brought her into the school. A white woman came through with her little girl and brought her into the school. After the white woman dropped off her little girl, she came outside and joined the mob. Everyone was afraid. What would happen to the white children in integration? It was terrible. They were frightened something awful. Late that afternoon the white girl came home. "What happened?" her mother asked anxiously. "What happened with you and the colored girl?" The little white girl looked at her mother. "We were both so scared," she said, "we sat and held hands all day."

    ➤BILL WHITE,
       former first baseman for the St. Louis Cardinals,
       as quoted in an article titled "Bill White: A Man Must Say
         What He Thinks Is Right," from *Sport*, July 1964

I don't think anyone in or out of sports could ever seriously accuse Willie Mays of offending white sensitivities. But when he was in California, whites refused to sell him a house in their community. They loved his talent, but they didn't want him for a neighbor.

    ➤JACKIE ROBINSON,
       first African-American baseball player in the major leagues,
       in *I Never Had It Made: An Autobiography* by Jackie Robinson,
         as told to Alfred Duckett, 1972

Racism is not an excuse to not do the best you can.

    ➤ARTHUR ASHE,
       Hall of Fame tennis player and AIDS activist,
       as quoted in *Sports Illustrated*, July 1991.

I know I got it made while the masses of black people are catchin' hell, but as long as they ain't free, I ain't free.

~Muhammad Ali,
   Olympic gold medalist and former world heavyweight champion,
   as quoted in *Playboy,* **1975**

I don't think that baseball should be particularly proud of this day. It's been long overdue.

~Bowie Kuhn,
   former major league baseball commissioner,
   on Frank Robinson being named the first African-American manager in the major leagues,
   as quoted in *Five Seasons* **by Roger Angell, 1982**

I wasn't invited up to shake hands with Hitler—but I wasn't invited to the White House to shake hands with the president, either.

~Jesse Owens,
   the greatest sprinter of his generation, after winning four gold medals at the Berlin Olympics in 1936, then being refused entrance through the front door of the Waldorf-Astoria Hotel, where a reception was being held in his honor

It was a very tough year. I was really rebelling. I considered myself a racist at that time. Basically, I was against all white people.

~Michael Jordan,
   former NBA superstar with the Chicago Bulls,
   referring to a period during his teenage years when he was very angry at whites after seeing *Roots,* **the television series about black history and slavery,**
   as quoted in *Playboy,* **May 1992**

I look back in amazement now that we ever tolerated a day without the blacks in the big leagues. Looking back, I can't understand how it never struck me as odd that I went through school without ever having a black in class. And I'd competed against just one, who couldn't hit a curve ball . . . but, then, hell, I couldn't either.

~Bob Broeg,
   sportswriter, editor, columnist, and author,
   in *The National Pastime,* **Fall 1982**

Reading

I don't read fiction. I read other stuff, about atomic bombs and "I Was a Prisoner of the Reds," stuff like that. You can learn something from them. When I was a kid, I used to read fiction. In the stories, the fellow would always hit a home run in the ninth inning to win the game. Since then, I have found out that things don't happen that way in real life. So I don't read fiction anymore.

— GEORGE SHUBA,
   former major league baseball player,
   quoted in *The Sporting News*, April 27, 1955, while Shuba
      was playing for the Los Angeles Dodgers

Math and science are my favorite subjects. Literature is my least favorite, which is strange because I really like some books. But dusty old tomes like *Wuthering Heights* are just not my style.

— TARA LIPINSKI,
   Olympic gold medalist and world figure skating champion,
   in her autobiography, *Tara Lipinski: Triumph on Ice*, with
      Emily Costello, 1998

Reading isn't good for a ballplayer. Not good for his eyes. If my eyes went bad even a little bit I couldn't hit home runs. So I gave up reading.

— BABE RUTH,
   legendary Hall of Fame outfielder,
   when a reporter asked him what books he was reading,
   as quoted in *Babe: The Legend Comes to Life* by Robert W.
      Creamer, 1974

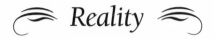

Reality

Every man's got to figure to get beat sometime.

—Joe Louis,
former world heavyweight champion,
as quoted in *The Ultimate Success Quotations Library*, Cyber
Nation International, Inc., Reno, NV, 1997

In all honesty, nobody knows what the hell is going on.

—Bob Clarke,
Hall of Fame player with the Philadelphia Flyers and their
general manager,
referring to a series of events that occurred within the
National Hockey League,
as quoted in *Sports Illustrated*, December 22, 1997

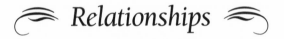

Relationships

When we won the league championship, all the married guys on
the club had to thank their wives for putting up with all the stress
and strain all season. I had to thank all the single broads in New
York.

—Joe Namath,
Hall of Fame quarterback with the New York Jets,
as quoted in news summaries, December 31, 1979

I got along with him fine. He only suspended me once for two
weeks. It was on account of I socked him.

—Al Bridwell,
former New York Giants shortstop,
referring to his relationship with Giant manager John
McGraw

Steve has to take advantage of his peak earning years, but God, sometimes I just wish I had someone to cuddle with. Baseball wives are told how lucky we are, and we're not ungrateful. But I have to have someone to talk to at night. Steve is gone 92 days a year. In the offseason, he's busy with business affairs. Sometimes you just crave conversation.

—CYNDY GARVEY,
 ex-wife of former major league baseball player Steve Garvey,
 as quoted in *High Inside: Memoirs of a Baseball Wife* by
  Danielle Gagnon Torrez, 1993

Belonging to a baseball club is like being a member of a social club, Rotary or the Knights of Columbus. Only more so. Instead of dropping in every Wednesday night to listen to the minutes of the last meeting and shoot some pool, you are out with the boys every night. In other ways, however, a ballclub is nothing at all like a social club. Players are from widely differing backgrounds and have widely differing outside interests. If not for this one common bond, an ability to play baseball better than almost anybody else in the country, it is rather unlikely that any two of us would ever have met. But the differences mean nothing. There is, among us, a far closer relationship than the purely social one of a fraternal organization because we are bound together not only by a single interest but by a common goal. To win. Nothing else matters, and nothing else will do.

—SANDY KOUFAX,
 Hall of Fame pitcher for the Los Angeles Dodgers,
 in "What Baseball Means to Me," by Sandy Koufax with Ed
  Linn, in *Look* magazine, July 26, 1966

I realized how much our relationship had deepened after I left baseball. It was that later relationship that made me feel almost as if I had lost my own father. Branch Rickey, especially after I was no longer in the sports spotlight, treated me like a son.

—JACKIE ROBINSON,
 first African-American baseball player in the major leagues,
 referring to Rickey, the general manager who brought him to
  the Brooklyn Dodgers, after Rickey's death,
 as quoted in *I Never Had It Made: An Autobiography* by Jackie
  Robinson, as told to Alfred Duckett, 1972

Respect

I'm not concerned with your liking or disliking me . . . All I ask is that you respect me as a human being.

⟶JACKIE ROBINSON,
    first African-American baseball player to play in the major
        leagues,
    as quoted in *Grand Slams and Fumbles* by Peter Beilenson, 1989

Lots of leaders want to be popular. I never cared about that. I want to be respected.

⟶DON SHULA,
    Hall of Fame coach of the Baltimore Colts and Miami
        Dolphins and the winningest NFL coach of all-time,
    in *The Book of Football Wisdom*, edited by Criswell Freeman,
        1996

Retirement

Watching Larry out on the court, I said to myself, "I used to be like that." If I can't give this team that kind of enthusiasm, I should get out.

⟶DEAN SMITH,
    legendary former basketball coach at the University of North
        Carolina,
    comparing himself to Larry Brown, a younger coach and one
        of his former players, while contemplating his retirement,
    as quoted in *Sports Illustrated*, October 20, 1997

You can only milk a cow so long, then you're left holding the pail.

⟶HANK AARON,
    Hall of Fame outfielder and all-time home run king,
    when announcing his retirement in 1976

Retire to what? I'm a golfer and a fisherman. I've got no place to retire to.

➤ JULIUS BOROS,
professional golfer,
as quoted in *Golfers on Golf*, edited by Downs MacRury, 1979

Dean old friend . . . please say it ain't so!

➤ A sign posted outside of Sutton's Drug Store in Chapel Hill,
North Carolina, on October 9, 1997, the day that longtime
University of North Carolina basketball coach Dean Smith
announced that he would retire

I wanted you to be the first to hear of my retirement.

➤ BOB MATHIAS,
the first two-time Olympic decathlon champion who won his
first gold medal at age 17,
to his brother, following Mathias' victory at the 1952 Olympic
games in Helsinki at age 21

I could ask the Phillies to keep me on to add to my statistics but my love for the game won't let me do that.

➤ MIKE SCHMIDT,
Hall of Fame third baseman for the Philadelphia Phillies,
referring to his sudden decision to retire when he was known
as one of the best players of the day

I look at the kids over here, and the way they're playing and the way they're fighting for themselves, and that says one thing to me: "Willie, it's time to say good-bye to America."

➤ WILLIE MAYS,
Hall of Fame outfielder, referring to the New York Mets' bench,
on his last day as a Met in Shea Stadium in 1973

I'm going to watch the grass grow and then go cut it.

➤ MICHAEL JORDAN,
former NBA superstar with the Chicago Bulls,
when announcing his retirement the first time in October 1993

I can't play any more. I can't hit the ball when I need to. I can't steal second when I need to. I can't go from first to third when I need to. I can't score from second when I need to. I have to quit.

➤ MICKEY MANTLE,
    legendary New York Yankees outfielder and Hall of Famer,
    explaining why he was retiring in 1968

I've got a lot of years to live after baseball. And I would like to live them with the complete use of my body.

➤ SANDY KOUFAX,
    Hall of Fame pitcher for the Los Angeles Dodgers,
    announcing his retirement on November 18, 1966

I don't want to be in your future. It's frustrating enough being in your present.

➤ ROGER ERICKSON,
    New York Yankees pitcher who retired after being demoted to
        the Yankees farm team;
    as quoted in *Sports Illustrated*, May 2, 1983

When they start hitting back at you, it's time to quit.

➤ HENRY RANSOM,
    professional golfer,
    after a ball ricocheted off a cliff and hit him

I told you fellows last spring I thought this would be my last year. I only wish I could have had a better year. But even if I hit .350, this would have been the last year for me. You all know I have had more than my share of physical injuries and setbacks during my career. In recent years these have been much too frequent to laugh off. When baseball is no longer fun it's no longer a game. And so, I've played my last game of ball.

➤ JOE DiMAGGIO,
    legendary New York Yankees outfielder and Hall of Famer,
    as quoted in *The Sporting News*, December 19, 1951

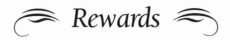

Rewards

I've always believed that if you put in the work, the results will come.

MICHAEL JORDAN,
former NBA superstar with the Chicago Bulls,
as quoted in *I Can't Accept Not Trying: Michael Jordan on the Pursuit of Excellence*, 1994

Risk

Soloing is serious business, because you can be seriously dead.

JOHN BACHAR,
rock climbing,
as quoted in *Newsweek*, October 1, 1984
in response to a question about climbing sheer rock faces
without mechanical aid

Rules

What you see here
What you hear here
What you say here
Let it stay here
When you leave here.

The Clubhouse Credo, supposedly unwritten, but posted on
many clubhouse walls

Be on time. Bust your butt. Play smart. And have some laughs while you're at it.

> ← WHITEY HERZOG, former major league manager, widely quoted
> at the time he resigned as manager of the St. Louis Cardinals
> in July 1990

1. Surround yourself with people who can't live without football.
2. Recognize winners. They come in all forms.
3. Have a plan for everything.

> ← PAUL "BEAR" BRYANT,
> legendary University of Alabama football coach,
> as quoted in *The Book of Football Wisdom*, edited by Criswell
> Freeman, 1996

For the benefit of you younger fellows, we have a lot of rules on this club. Midnight curfew, stay out of the bar at the hotel where we're staying, wear a shirt and sweater to breakfast and a coat and tie to dinner. Think you can remember all that?

> ← HANK BAUER,
> former manager of the Baltimore Orioles,
> as quoted in *The Sporting News*, April 1, 1967

Learn the fundamentals.
Study and work at the game as if it were a science.
Keep in top physical condition.
Make yourself as effective as possible.
Get the desire to win.
Keeping in the best physical condition and having an intense
spirit to succeed is the combination for winning games.

> ← TY COBB,
> legendary baseball player, manager, and Hall of Famer's "Six
> Keys to Baseball Success,"
> as quoted in *The Sporting News*, February 20, 1957

I believe in rules. Sure I do. If there weren't any rules, how could you break them?

> ← LEO DUROCHER,
> Hall of Fame manager of the Brooklyn Dodgers,
> as quoted in *The Speaker's Electronic Reference Collection*,
> Aapex Software, 1994

The fewer rules a coach has, the fewer rules there are for players to break.

> ━JOHN MADDEN,
> coach of the Oakland Raiders from 1969 to 1979, turned sportscaster,
> as quoted in *The Book of Football Wisdom*, edited by Criswell Freeman, 1996

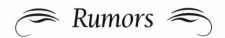 *Rumors*

I've discovered that the less I say, the more rumors I start.

> ━BOB CLARKE,
> former Philadelphia Flyers center and later their general manager,
> as quoted in *Sports Illustrated*, July 15, 1984

A woman asked me the other day if there's any truth to the rumor that Charlie Finley is out to get me. I said, "Honey, that ain't no rumor."

> ━BOWIE KUHN,
> former major league baseball commissioner,
> as quoted in *The Sporting News*, June 24, 1978

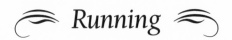 *Running*

Hitting the ball was easy. Running around the bases was the tough part.

> ━MICKEY MANTLE,
> legendary New York Yankees outfielder and Hall of Famer,
> as quoted in *Slick: My Life in and around Baseball* by Whitey Ford, 1987

There ain't a left-hander in the world who can run a straight line. It's the gravitational pull on the earth's axis that gets 'em.

—RAY MILLER,
former major league pitching coach,
referring to the difference between right-handed and left-handed pitchers

Well sir, I grew up in Oklahoma and out there, once you start running, there ain't nothing to stop you.

—PEPPER MARTIN,
former major league baseball player,
answering the question of how he learned to run so fast,
as quoted in *Baseball's Greatest Quotations*, by Paul Dickson, 1991

He makes his living running fast and I make mine running slow.

—BARRY BONDS,
outfielder for the Pittsburgh Pirates and San Francisco Giants,
comparing himself to Carl Lewis while referring to his slow home run trot around the bases,
as quoted in *The Major League Baseball Newsletter*, June 1990

My head was exploding, my stomach ripping, and even the tips of my fingers ached. The only thing I could think was, "if I live, I will never run again."

—TOM COURTNEY,
U.S. 1956 Olympic gold medalist,
as quoted in *Life*, Summer 1984

I sometimes think that running has given me a glimpse of the greatest freedom a man can ever know, because it results in the simultaneous liberation of both body and mind.

—SIR ROGER GILBERT BANNISTER,
English athlete and neurologist, who ran the first mile in less than four minutes in 1954,
as quoted in *The First Four Minutes*, 1955

I'm not crazy about running. I just do it to keep in shape for fishing.

— DONALD GOWDY,
66-year-old winner of the five-kilometer run at the 1997
North Carolina Senior State Games,
as quoted in *Sports Illustrated*, November 17, 1997

Sacrifice

Some guys aren't sacrificing. Until everyone wants to sacrifice, we'll be good, but we're not going to be a championship team.

— SCOTT STEVENS,
captain of the New Jersey Devils hockey team,
as quoted in the *San Francisco Examiner*, December 29, 1999

Sailing and Sailors

Sailing is just the bottom line, like adding up the score in bridge. My real interest is in the tremendous game of life.

— DENNIS CONNER,
yachtsman,
as quoted in *Time*, February 9, 1987

Even when we did win, we were using a rifle against a club . . . It's our sunburned minds. We need more Crocodile Dundees down here.

— BEN LEXCEN,
Australian yachtsman,
on winning the America's Cup in 1983,
as quoted in the *New York Times*, February 3, 1987

Design has taken the place of what sailing used to be.

➤ DENNIS CONNER,
yachtsman,
as quoted in *Time*, February 9, 1987

We don't have any sailors in Australia, we have rowers.

➤ BEN LEXCEN,
Australian yachtsman,
commenting on the U.S. victory at the America's Cup races,
as quoted in the *New York Times*, February 3, 1987

Scholarship

I'm glad it happened in front of the library. I've always emphasized scholarship.

➤ DOUG WEAVER,
former Kansas State University football coach,
on being hanged in effigy,
as quoted in *Sports Illustrated*, June 9, 1986

It was like a heart transplant. We tried to implant college in him, but his head rejected it.

➤ BARRY SWITZER,
former University of Oklahoma football coach,
referring to a player who dropped out of school,
as quoted in *Sports Illustrated*, November 12, 1973

Self-Confidence

You've got to believe in yourself and have a persistent mindset of never giving up, never quitting. If you get any inclination of "You're not good enough," it kills you.

➤ KEENAN MCCARDELL,
Jacksonville Jaguars wide receiver,
as quoted in the *Hartford Courant*, January 15, 2000

I was so concentrated. Nothing could interfere. I knew the whole way through, "Yeah, I'm going to kick some butt." There was no doubt in my mind I could do it.

➤ MICHELLE KWAN,
figure skating champion,
after winning the 1996 World Championships in Edmonton,
Canada,
as quoted in *Born to Skate: The Michelle Kwan Story* by
Edward Z. Epstein, 1997

If you're going to take gambles, you must have one thing: self-confidence.

➤ DON SHULA,
Hall of Fame head coach of the Baltimore Colts and Miami
Dolphins, and the winningest coach of all-time,
as quoted in *The Book of Football Wisdom*, edited by Criswell
Freeman, 1996

It's not going to be a situation of "Can I?" It's "I'm going to."

➤ SEAN ELLIOTT,
San Antonio Spurs forward,
referring to returning to the team after a kidney transplant six
months earlier,
as quoted in the *Fort Worth Star-Telegram*, January 16, 2000

I came to the Olympics to beat everything in sight, and that's just what I'm going to do.

➤ BABE DIDRIKSON ZAHARIAS,
Hall of Fame golfer and Olympic champion,
before the 1932 Olympic Games

Self-Improvement

If you're serious about improving your play, be brutally honest with yourself.

— GREG NORMAN,
   Australian golfer, also known as the "Great White Shark,"
   as quoted in *The Golfer's Book of Wisdom*, edited by Criswell
   Freeman, 1995

Sex

Sex is a very significant aspect of athlete's lives. If you think about it, you realize right away that athletic performance and sexual performance always go hand in hand.

— MAURY ALLEN,
   author and sportswriter,
   as quoted in *Late Innings* by Roger Angell, 1982

Bullpen conversations cover the gambit of male bull sessions. Sex, religion, politics, sex. Full circle. Occasionally, the game—or business—of baseball intrudes.

— JIM BROSNAN,
   former major league baseball player,
   in his book *The Long Season*, 1981

I was monogamous at a time when a lot of friends were not. I was never one to hop around, to date this girl on Friday and that girl on Saturday . . . Sex wasn't something that was a main interest to me, either.

— STEVE GARVEY,
   former major league baseball player,
   from his autobiography *Garvey*, 1986;
   the remark was often repeated when Garvey's sexual exploits
      became common tabloid news in late 1989 and 1990

Being with a woman all night never hurt no professional baseball player. It's staying up all night looking for a woman that does him in.

➤CASEY STENGEL,
   former manager of the New York Yankees and New York Mets,
   widely quoted

Hitting is better than sex.

➤REGGIE JACKSON,
   former major league baseball player,
   as quoted in *Esquire*, March 1, 1978

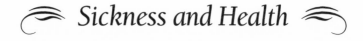 *Sickness and Health*

I will tell you privately it's not going to get better, it's going to get worse all the time, but don't fret. Remember, we "play the ball where it lies," and now let's not talk about this, ever again.

➤BOBBY JONES,
   Hall of Fame golfer,
   after being diagnosed with a rare disease while in his mid-40s

I'm not going to be stupid about this heart condition, but I'm not going to live my whole life in fear of this thing, either. If it goes, it goes.

➤LARRY BIRD,
   former Boston Celtics star and coach of the Indiana Pacers,
      who suffers from an irregular heartbeat,
   as quoted in *Sports Illustrated*, September 6, 1999

I've been healthy my whole career except for nagging injuries the last few years.

➤MIKE SMITH,
   former major league baseball player,
   as quoted in the *Washington Post*, March 9, 1986

I always knew there was something funny about my heart.

━━Larry Bird,
  former Boston Celtics star and coach of the Indiana Pacers,
    who suffers from an irregular heartbeat,
  as quoted in *Sports Illustrated*, September 6, 1999

My health is good enough above the shoulders.

━━Casey Stengel,
  former manager of the New York Yankees and New York Mets,
  when asked about his health after taking over the Mets,
  as quoted in *The Incredible Mets* by Maury Allen, 1969

Friends, relatives, peers, classmates; they were all dying. I had no indication of any trouble, but I began to get a fear of developing heart disease. I knew there was a better way to live, and I knew it was about time I did something about it.

━━Dr. Paul Spangler,
  who at age 92 ran and completed the New York City
    marathon,
  referring to why he started running at age 69,
  as quoted in *December Champions* by Bob Darden and W.R.
    Spence, M.D., 1993

If you don't do what's best for your body, you're the one who comes up on the short end.

━━Julius Erving,
  Hall of Fame basketball player,
  as quoted in *Get Lost Adventure Magazine*

Thank you very much, ladies and gentlemen. You know how bad my voice sounds. Well, it feels just as bad . . . There's been so many lovely things said about me, I'm glad I had the opportunity to thank everybody. Thank you.

━━Babe Ruth,
  legendary Hall of Fame outfielder,
  during "Babe Ruth Day" at Yankee Stadium on April 27, 1947,
    at which the seriously ill Ruth was recognized and honored
    by 58,339 fans, who gave him the greatest ovation ever
    known to baseball

You have to get knocked down to realize how people really feel about you. I've realized that more than ever lately. The other day, I was on my way to the car. It was hailing, the streets were slippery, and I was having a tough time of it. I came to a corner and started to slip. But before I could fall, four people jumped out of nowhere to help me. When I thanked them, they all said they knew about my illness and had been keeping an eye on me.

> ►LOU GEHRIG,
> Hall of Fame first baseman for the New York Yankees,
> shortly before his death in 1941 from amyotrophic lateral
> sclerosis, better known as Lou Gehrig's disease,
> as quoted in *Sport*, October 1948

Suffering is overrated. It doesn't teach you anything.

> ►BILL VEECK,
> son of the owner of the Chicago Cubs, who brought African-
> American players Satchel Paige and Larry Doby into the
> majors; known for his controversial opinions on many sub-
> jects,
> referring to his many operations and sicknesses,
> as quoted in the *Washington Post*, May 31, 1981

I never have been sick. I don't even know what it means to be sick. I hear other players say they have a cold. I just don't know what it would be like to have a cold—I never had one.

> ►HONUS WAGNER,
> Hall of Fame shortstop, who played for more than 35 years,
> as quoted in *Baseball as I Have Known It* by Fred G. Lieb, 1976

I honestly don't know anyone who wants to live more than I do. It is a driving wish that is always with me these days, a wish that only a person who has been close to death can know and understand.

> ►BABE RUTH,
> legendary Hall of Fame outfielder,
> after being diagnosed with cancer, from which he died in 1948

The termites have got me.

> ►BABE RUTH,
> legendary Hall of Fame outfielder,
> to Connie Mack on the day before Ruth died of cancer in 1948

None of us loves having it. And, as much as you want to knock down the ignorant misconceptions of those who think it's freaky and weird, you don't want epilepsy to be read into every argument you have with the umpires. "Look at Buddy. Is he going to lose it?" One reason I never wanted people to know was just that I didn't want them to worry about me. I don't think about it every day. I don't think about it every month. I'd be the same way without it.

> ━BUDDY BELL,
> former major league baseball player and manager,
> referring to the epilepsy that he had for 15 years while
>   playing ball,
> as quoted in the *Washington Post*, November 5, 1989

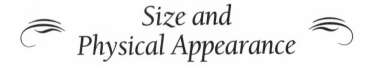

Size and Physical Appearance

Even when I was little, I was big.

> ━WILLIAM "THE REFRIGERATOR" PERRY,
> Chicago Bears defensive tackle,
> as quoted in *Life*, January 1986

I guess you could say I'm the redemption of the fat man. A guy will be watching me on TV and see that I don't look in any better shape than he is. "Hey, Maude," he'll holler. "Get a load of this guy. And he's a 20-game winner."

> ━MICKEY LOLICH,
> former Detroit Tigers pitcher,
> as quoted in *Sports Illustrated*, June 19, 1972

I don't need a chest protector. I need a bra.

> ━GUS TRIANDOS,
> former catcher for the Baltimore Orioles,
> playing at an Old-Timers game

My mother had to send me to the movies with my birth certificate, so that I wouldn't have to pay the extra 50 cents [that adults had to pay].

— KAREEM ABDUL-JABBAR,
Hall of Fame basketball player who at 7 feet, 1 ⅜ inches dominated professional basketball in the 1970s and early 1980s,
as quoted in *Jet*, March 19, 1984

Nobody roots for Goliath.

— WILT CHAMBERLAIN,
Hall of Fame basketball player who was just over 7 feet tall,
as quoted in the *Guinness Dictionary of Sports Quotations* by Colin Jarman, 1990

He's too slick, too smart, too preppy, he doesn't even look like a race car driver.

— A fan at the UAW-GM Quality 500 race on October 5, 1997, referring to driver Jeff Gordon,
as quoted in *Sports Illustrated*, November 17, 1997

A heck of a lot better than being the smallest player in the minors.

— FRED PATEK,
a 5-foot, 5 ¼-inch-Kansas City Royals shortstop,
when asked how it felt to be the smallest player in the major leagues

A big player has to prove he can't play; a little one has to prove that he can.

— LEN MERULLO,
a scout for the Chicago Cubs,
as quoted in *Baseball Digest*, June 1961

We don't have any refrigerators. We have a few pot-belly stoves, but they're on the coaching staff.

— DAVE CURREY,
University of Cincinnati football coach,
referring to Chicago Bears defensive tackle William "the Refrigerator" Perry,
as quoted in *Sports Illustrated*, December 2, 1985

He looks like a pair of pliers.

—JOHNNY BENCH,
> legendary Hall of Fame catcher for the Cincinnati Reds,
> referring to baseball player Von Hayes while broadcasting a
> game,
> as quoted in *Sports Illustrated*, August 18, 1988

The way to make coaches think you're in shape in the spring is to get a tan.

—WHITEY FORD,
> New York Yankees Hall of Fame pitcher,
> as quoted in *Ball Four* by Jim Bouton, 1970

Some people call me the Kitchen, some call me the Dining Room— and some call me the Cafeteria!

—WILLIAM "THE REFRIGERATOR" PERRY,
> Chicago Bears defensive tackle,
> as quoted on NBC television, September 23, 1986

So I'm ugly. So what? I never saw anyone hit with his face.

—YOGI BERRA,
> Hall of Fame catcher for the New York Yankees,
> as quoted in *The Book of Sport Quotes* by B.R. Sugar, 1979

Until I saw (Mickey) Mantle peel down for his shower in the club-house at Comiskey Park one afternoon, I never knew how he developed his brutal power, but his bare back looked like a barrel-ful of snakes.

—DALE LANCASTER,
> sports columnist,
> referring to Mickey Mantle,
> as quoted in *Baseball Stars of 1963*, edited by Ray Robinson,
> 1963

I use my muscles as a conversation piece, like someone walking a cheetah down 42nd Street.

—ARNOLD SCHWARZENEGGER,
> bodybuilder and actor,
> as quoted in various news summaries, December 31, 1979

Golf is a great game to play when you're pregnant. It's a gentle form of exercise, and if you play regularly it can help you avoid gaining too much weight.

    ━NANCY LOPEZ,
        Hall of Fame golfer,
        as quoted in *Golfers on Golf,* **edited by Downs MacRury, 1997**

I have stubby hands with short fingers . . . Actually my wife, Barbara, has stronger hands than mine from doing dishes . . . Knowing that, you won't be surprised to learn that I regard as bunk that hoary old maxim about big, strong hands being essential for good golf.

    ━JACK NICKLAUS,
        Hall of Fame golfer and winner of 20 major championships,
        as quoted in *Golfers on Golf,* **edited by Downs MacRury, 1997**

Skiing

Skiing is a battle against yourself, always to the frontiers of the impossible. But most of all, it must give you pleasure. It is not an obligation but a joy.

    ━JEAN-CLAUDE KILLY,
        Olympic gold medalist and world ski champion,
        as quoted in *Sports Illustrated,* **November 18, 1968**

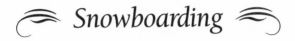 *Snowboarding*

Snowboarding is about fresh tracks and carving powder and being yourself and not being judged by others. It's not about nationalism and politics and big money.

— TERJE HAAKONSEN,
  Norwegian snowboarder,
   referring to snowboarding being included as sport in the
     1998 Olympics Games,
  as quoted in *Sports Illustrated*, December 22, 1997

 *Spirituality*

I've never been to heaven and, thinkin' back on my life, I probably won't get a chance to go. I guess the Masters is as close as I'm going to get.

— FUZZY ZOELLER,
  professional golfer and winner of the 1979 Masters,
  as quoted in *Golfers on Golf*, edited by Downs MacRury, 1997

I don't see any spiritual, religious drive to it. I suppose, deep down underneath, I count my blessings, if you will, that I am able to do this. And I recognize that somewhere there is a Supreme Being who is looking after me and taking care of me. But is He helping me to finish the Ironman Triathlon? I don't know. I think much more in down-to-earth ways.

— NORTON DAVEY,
  an Ocean Hill, California man, who at age 74 was one of the
    world's best Ironman triathletes,
  as quoted in *December Champions* by Bob Darden and W.R.
    Spence, M.D., 1993

I believe in an extra-consciousness that looks after you. It only comes into play in extreme circumstances, which for me is in the mountains. That's where I fit in best.

➤ ROGER MARSHALL,
   mountain climber,
   as quoted in the *New York Times*, August 10, 1986

 *Sportsmanship*

One man practicing sportsmanship is better than a hundred teaching it.

➤ KNUTE ROCKNE,
   football coach who's credited with establishing Notre Dame as
      a football powerhouse,
   as quoted on the Creative Quotations website

Before we even say a word about the game, let's get down on our knees and pray for Coach Paterno's son.

➤ FRANK MALONEY,
   Syracuse University coach,
   to his team after losing to Penn State in 1977; Paterno missed
      the game because one of his sons had been seriously
      injured and was hospitalized,
   as quoted in *Paterno: By the Book* by Joe Paterno with Bernard
      Asbell, 1989

Sports

Sport must be amateur or it is not sport. Sports played profession-
ally are entertainment.

➤AVERY BRUNDAGE,
president of the International Olympic Committee,
as quoted in *This Week,* January 14, 1968

Statistics

We're not the Os anymore. We're the 1s.

➤FRANK ROBINSON,
the first African-American manager in the major leagues,
referring to the first win of the season by his team, the Baltimore Orioles, after 21 losses,
as quoted in "Memorable Quotes of 1988," *Tampa Tribune*,
December 25, 1988

Strategy

Float like a butterfly, sting like a bee.

➤MUHAMMAD ALI,
Olympic gold medalist and former world heavyweight champion,
as quoted on the Creative Quotations website

In baseball, my theory is to strive for consistency, not to worry about the "numbers." If you dwell on statistics, you get short-sighted; if you aim for consistency, the numbers will be there at the end. My job isn't to strike guys out, it's to get them out, sometimes by striking them out.

➤ TOM SEAVER,
   Hall of Fame pitcher, turned broadcaster,
   as quoted in the *New York Times*, January 11, 1976

You can talk about strategy all you want, but what really matters is resiliency.

➤ HALE IRWIN,
   professional golfer,
   as quoted in *Golfers on Golf*, edited by Downs MacRury, 1997

I'll let the racket do the talking.

➤ JOHN MCENROE,
   Hall of Fame tennis player, U.S. Davis Cup captain and
      broadcaster,
   on defending his title as Wimbledon champion,
   as quoted in the *London Times*, June 26, 1984

If you're up against a girl with big boobs, bring her to the net and make her hit backhand volleys.

➤ BILLIE JEAN KING,
   Hall of Fame tennis player and activist for women's rights,
   in her book *Billie Jean King*, 1982

How to hit home runs: I swing as hard as I can, and I try to swing right through the ball. In boxing, your fist usually stops when you hit a man, but it's possible to hit so hard that your fist doesn't stop. I try to follow through in the same way. The harder you grip the bat, the more you can swing it through the ball, and the farther the ball will go. I swing big, with everything I've got. I hit big or I miss big. I like to live as big as I can.

➤ BABE RUTH,
   legendary Hall of Fame outfielder,
   as quoted in *Words of Wisdom* by William Safire and Leonard
      Safire, 1989

When in doubt, punt!

> ◄—JOHN HEISMAN,
>> legendary college football coach and namesake of the Heisman Trophy, who is credited with legalizing the forward pass and originating the center snap and the count signals of the quarterback,
>> as quoted in *The Book of Football Wisdom*, edited by Criswell Freeman, 1996

When you find your opponent's weak spot, hammer it.

> ◄—JOHN HEISMAN,
>> college football coach and namesake of the Heisman Trophy, who's credited with legalizing the forward pass and originating the center snap and the count signals of the quarterback,
>> as quoted in *The Book of Football Wisdom*, edited by Criswell Freeman, 1996

Take things as they are. Punch when you have to punch. Kick when you have to kick.

> ◄—BRUCE LEE,
>> U.S. martial arts expert,
>> from *The Ultimate Success Quotations Library*, Cyber Nation International, Inc., Reno, NV, 1997

⪦ *Strength* ⪧

Derrick said, "Coach, be strong." He never told me how strong I needed to be.

> ◄—GUNTHER CUNNINGHAM,
>> coach of the Kansas City Chiefs,
>> of the last time he spoke with Chiefs linebacker Derrick Thomas before Thomas' death on February 8, 2000

Success

I've had enough success for two lifetimes, My success is talent put together with hard work and luck.

— KAREEM ABDUL-JABBAR,
   Hall of Fame basketball player,
   in *Star*, May 1986

Sweat plus sacrifice equals success.

— CHARLIE FINLEY,
   former owner of the Oakland Athletics,
   as quoted in *Get Lost Adventure Magazine*

I was not successful as a ballplayer, as it was a game of skill.

— CASEY STENGEL,
   former manager of the New York Yankees and New York Mets,
   recalled on his death, September 29, 1975

Baseball is the only field of endeavor where a man can succeed three times out of 10 and be considered a good performer.

— TED WILLIAMS,
   legendary Hall of Fame outfielder for the Boston Red Sox,
   widely quoted

About the only problem with success is that it does not teach you how to deal with failure.

— TOMMY LASORDA,
   former manager of the Los Angeles Dodgers,
   in his book *The Artful Dodger*, 1985

Success is a journey not a destination. The doing is usually more important than the outcome. Not everyone can be Number One.

— ARTHUR ASHE,
   Hall of Fame tennis player and AIDS activist,
   from *The Ultimate Success Quotations Library*, Cyber Nation
      International, Inc., Reno, NV, 1997

I know a lot of people say when they succeed, suddenly it's like throwing off a huge weight, but I enjoy it so much. Well, not like it's exactly fun, not birthday-party fun, but I love it so, I do.

➤MICHAEL JOHNSON,
    Olympic champion sprinter,
    referring to his rigorous training schedule and the pressure he
      puts on himself,
    after setting a new world record and winning the 200-meter
      dash in the 1996 Olympic games in Atlanta

The secret to my success was clean living and a fast-moving out-field.

➤LEFTY GOMEZ,
    Hall of Fame pitcher for the New York Yankees during the
      1930s,
    as quoted in the *New York Times*, April 25, 1976

The formula for success is simple: practice and concentration then more practice and more concentration.

➤BABE DIDRIKSON ZAHARIAS,
    Hall of Fame golfer and Olympic champion,
    as quoted in *The Golfer's Book of Wisdom*, edited by Criswell
      Freeman, 1995

Success is peace of mind which is a direct result of self-satisfaction in knowing you did your best to become the best that you are capable of becoming.

➤JOHN WOODEN,
    legendary UCLA basketball coach who led the Bruins to 10
      national championships,
    as quoted in *Sportswit* by Lee Green, 1984

People of mediocre ability sometimes achieve outstanding success because they don't know when to quit. Most men succeed because they are determined to.

➤GEORGE ALLEN,
    former coach of the Los Angeles Rams and Washington Red-
      skins, noted for his exceptional work ethic,
    as quoted in *The Ultimate Success Quotations Library*, Cyber
      Nation International, Inc., Reno, NV, 1997

Well, we knocked the bastard off!

    —EDMUND HILLARY,
        New Zealand mountain climber,
        after reaching the top of Mount Everest in 1953

Success isn't measured by money or power or social rank. Success is measured by your discipline and inner peace.

    —MIKE DITKA,
        Hall of Fame tight end and former head coach,
        as quoted in *The Book of Football Wisdom*, edited by Criswell
           Freeman, 1996

Support

She hasn't missed a race in 20 years. She does the timing. For most of the races we've gone to the last five years, there's another couple goes along to help. But before that, my wife and I would go alone. And if I have to change an engine or transmission, she knows which end of a wrench is the business end.

    —JOSEPH HAUSER JR.,
        an Odenton, Maryland, race car driver who at age 73 boasted
           120 victories between 1969 and 1992,
        as quoted in *December Champions* by Bob Darden and W.R.
           Spence, M.D., 1993

Swearing

The thing about sport, any sport, is that swearing is very much part of it.

—JIMMY GREAVES,
English football player,
attributed 1989

All pro athletes are bilingual. They speak English and profanity.

—GORDIE HOWE,
legendary Hall of Fame hockey player,
dismissing Canadian bilingualism,
as quoted in the *Toronto Star*, May 27, 1975

Things were changing fast by that time. Women were beginning to come to the ball parks. We hadda stop cussin'.

—HONUS WAGNER,
Hall of Fame shortstop who played for more than 35 years,
as quoted in *Sport*, June 1949

Judas Priest!

—BRANCH RICKEY,
baseball innovator and president-general manager for the
Brooklyn Dodgers;
this was the closest he came to swearing, the phrase became
something of a trademark

Talent — and Lack of Same

You've got a hundred more young kids than you have a place for on your club. Every one of 'em has had a goin' away party. They been given the shaving kit and the $50. They kissed everybody and said, "See you in the majors in two years." You see these poor kids who shouldn't even be there in the first place. You write on the report card "4-4-4- and out." That's the lowest rating in everything. Then you call 'em in and say, "It's the consensus among us that we're going to let you go back home." Some of them cry. Some get mad. But none of 'em will leave until you answer 'em one question: "Skipper, what do you think?" And you gotta look every one of those kids in the eye and kick their dreams in the ass and say no. If you say it mean enough, maybe they do themselves a favor and don't waste years learning what you can see in a day. They don't have what it takes to make the majors. Just like I never had it.

> ➤ EARL WEAVER,
> Hall of Fame manager of the Baltimore Orioles,
> as quoted in the *Washington Post*

Talent wins out.

> ➤ ALTHEA GIBSON,
> Hall of Fame tennis player, was the first African-American
> player to win the U.S. Open and Wimbledon championships,
> in *And I Quote* by Ashton Applewhite, 1992

The main thing to do is relax and let your talent do the work.

> ➤ CHARLES BARKLEY,
> named one of the 50 greatest players in NBA history,
> as quoted on NBC-TV, June 11, 1993

Hard work always beats talent.

—TRACE ARMSTRONG,
  defensive tackle for the Miami Dolphins,
  as quoted in the November 11, 1999, edition of the *Miami
  Herald*

Our strikers couldn't score in a brothel.

—TOMMY DOCHERTY,
  Scottish footballer and manager,
  referring to the forwards of the Wolverhampton Wanderers
  team, 1985

Teammates

Ask not what your teammates can do for you. Ask what you can do
for your teammates.

—MAGIC JOHNSON,
  former NBA superstar with the Los Angeles Lakers,
  as quoted in *Get Lost Adventure Magazine*

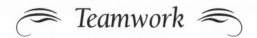

Teamwork

The point of the game is not how well the individual does but
whether the team wins. That is the beautiful heart of the game, the
blending of personalities, the mutual sacrifices for group success.

—BILL BRADLEY,
  Hall of Fame forward for the New York Knicks, U.S. Senator,
  presidential candidate,
  from his book *Life on the Run,* 1976

You can't win if you don't play as a unit.

➤KAREEM ABDUL-JABBAR,
Hall of Fame basketball player,
as quoted in *Star*, May 1968

Winning isn't as important as doing well individually. You can't take teamwork up to the front office to negotiate.

➤KEN LANDREAUX,
former Los Angeles Dodger outfielder,
as quoted in *Life*, January 1985

You almost must give these guys the opportunity to shine. But at the same time, my philosophy always has been if I'm going to go down, I want to go down shooting.

➤MICHAEL JORDAN,
former NBA superstar with the Chicago Bulls,
on his role as team leader,
as quoted in *Hoop* magazine, January 1985

We don't all have to be best friends, but we've got to play like we are.

➤MARCUS CAMBY,
forward for the New York Knicks,
as quoted in *Sports Illustrated*, February 7, 2000

Talent wins games, but teamwork and intelligence win championships.

➤MICHAEL JORDAN,
former NBA superstar with the Chicago Bulls,
as quoted in *I Can't Accept Not Trying: Michael Jordan on the Pursuit of Excellence*, 1994

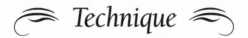

Technique

I let my feet spend as little time on the ground as possible. From the air, fast down, and from the ground, fast up.

— JESSE OWENS,
 the greatest sprinter of his generation, won four gold medals
  at the Berlin Olympics in 1936,
 as quoted in *The Guinness Dictionary of Sports Quotations*
  by Colin Jarman, 1990

I never had technique.

— AL OERTER,
 discus thrower and winner of four Olympic gold medals,
 as quoted in the *New York Times*, May 16, 1978

There's no secret. You just press the accelerator to the floor and steer left.

— BILL VUKOVICH,
 two-time winner of the Indianapolis 500,
 speaking about how he drives in the Indy race.

People ask me why I ride with my bottom in the air. Well, I've got to put it somewhere.

— LESTER KEITH PIGGOTT,
 English champion jockey,
 as quoted in *The Guinness Dictionary of Sports Quotations*
  by Colin Jarman, 1990

 *Tenacity*

If I give up, then they give up. No matter how sick or tired I was, I felt an obligation to the city and the team . . . I'm tired and I'm weak, but I have a whole summer to recuperate.

➤ MICHAEL JORDAN,
former NBA superstar with the Chicago Bulls,
following Game 5 of the 1997 NBA Finals in which he scored
38 points to help beat the Utah Jazz, despite a stomach
virus that made him so sick he nearly passed out

Anyone who thinks that I would resign doesn't know me very well. When I came here, I came here with the idea of winning a Super Bowl. That hasn't changed.

➤ NORV TURNER,
Washington Redskins head coach,
as stated January 1, 2000, during a rocky period with the
team's owner

 *Thanks*

Thank you, God, for giving me strength and making me a ballplayer.

➤ JIM "CATFISH" HUNTER,
Hall of Fame pitcher,
as quoted on Catfish Hunter Day at Yankee Stadium on
September 16, 1979

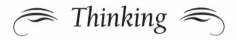 *Thinking*

Sometimes thinking too much can destroy your momentum.

—TOM WATSON,
Hall of Fame golfer,
in *The Golfer's Book of Wisdom,* edited by Criswell Freeman,
1995

There is a syndrome in sports called "paralysis by analysis."

—ARTHUR ASHE,
Hall of Fame tennis player and AIDS activist,
from *The Ultimate Success Quotations Library*, Cyber Nation
International, Inc., Reno, NV, 1997

If we're going to win the pennant, we've got to start thinking we're
not as good as we think we are.

—CASEY STENGEL,
former manager of the New York Yankees and New York Mets,
referring to his 1953 Yankees team

Thinking instead of acting is the number one disease in golf.

—SAM SNEAD,
Hall of Fame golfer and winner of a record 81 Professional
Golf Association tournaments,
as quoted in *The Golfer's Book of Wisdom*, edited by Criswell
Freeman, 1995

I want people to think of me as an iron man. I feel as strong physically as I did earlier in the season, but there have been times when
it's been tough mentally. You get tired of thinking and tired of concentrating, and then as you pop up or strike out, you say, "How did
I do that? I wasn't even thinking."

—CAL RIPKEN JR.,
Baltimore Orioles shortstop and holder of the major league
record for consecutive games played,
as quoted in *Sports Illustrated*, October 3, 1983

You can't think and hit at the same time.

➤YOGI BERRA,
  Hall of Fame catcher for the New York Yankees,
  as quoted *The Guinness Dictionary of Sports Quotations* by
    Colin Jarman, 1990

When you're playing poorly, you start thinking too much. That's when you confuse yourself.

➤GREG NORMAN,
  Australian golfer, also known as the "Great White Shark,"
  as quoted in *The Golfer's Book of Wisdom*, edited by Criswell
    Freeman, 1995

If you don't think too good, don't think too much.

➤TED WILLIAMS,
  legendary Hall of Fame outfielder for the Boston Red Sox,
  Friendly Advice, edited by Jon Winokur, 1990

The whole secret of mastering the game of golf—and this applies to the beginner as well as to the pro—is to cultivate a mental approach to the game that will enable you to shrug off the bad shots, shrug off the bad days, keep patient and know in your heart that sooner or later you will be back on top.

➤ARNOLD PALMER,
  Hall of Fame golfer,
  as quoted in *Golfers on Golf*, edited by Downs MacRury, 1997

 *Training*

If you train hard, you'll not only be hard, you'll be hard to beat.

➤HERSCHEL WALKER,
  former professional football player and Heisman Trophy
    winner,
  as quoted in *Get Lost Adventure Magazine*

I don't have a formal daily exercise routing. I keep doing every-thing I can. I have a philosophy that, if something gets hard, just do it! If you keep giving up on the hard things, of course, you keep giving up on more and more things as you get older. So I subscribe to the opposite: if it is difficult to do, do it.

⟵KEN BEER,
a Hillsborough, California tennis player, who since starting to play competitively at age 60 has won more than 70 national tournaments,
as quoted in *December Champions* by Bob Darden and W.R. Spence, M.D., 1993

Everyone has limits on the time they can devote to exercise, and cross-training simply gives you the best return on your investment— balanced fitness with minimum injury risk and maximum fun.

⟵PAULA NEWBY-FRASER,
eight-time winner of the Ironman Triathlon,
as quoted in *Get Lost Adventure Magazine*

I don't generally like running. I believe in training by rising gently up and down from the bench.

⟵SATCHEL PAIGE,
former Negro League star pitcher and one of the first African-Americans to play in the major leagues,
as quoted in *Out of My League* by George Plimpton, 1961

I compete in one Ironman Triathlon after another during the sea-son, so I use one to train for the next one. During the rest of the year, I use my legs and wheels to literally run errands, to church, to the post office. Of course, if the groceries are too heavy, I have to take a car. Otherwise, though, anything I can do either by running or biking, I do. It is not unusual for me to do a mini-triathlon as I go about my day, especially if it is one of the three or four days each week I also go swimming.

⟵SISTER MADONNA BUTLER,
a Spokane, Washington, Catholic nun, who at age 62 was setting records in Ironman Triathlon events,
as quoted in *December Champions* by Bob Darden and W.R. Spence, M.D., 1993

To break training without permission is an act of treason.

      —JOHN HEISMAN,
          college football coach and namesake of the Heisman Trophy,
              who is credited with legalizing the forward pass and
              originating the center snap and the count signals of the
              quarterback,
          as quoted in *The Book of Football Wisdom*, edited by Criswell
              Freeman, 1996

My exercise is that I rope three-four times a week at home. I've got my own arena and my own calves and some good horses. But I get a lot of exercise calf roping. This is about as good an exercise as you can get. I'm not in any better shape than I was when I first retired because of the roping, but I'm still in good shape—considering my age. Seventy-eight is getting on up there. I've always tried to stay in shape. I'll go in the house and sit on the couch and watch TV for an hour or two and I'll get to hurtin' all over and I've got to get up and get to movin' all around . . . I attribute my shape to working all my life, and staying active, and doing stuff.

      —ROY "TUFFY" OVERTURF,
          an Odessa, Texas, rodeo rider, who at age 78 dominated the
              1992 National Old-Timers Calf Roping Association's
              summer rodeos across Texas,
          as quoted in *December Champions* by Bob Darden and
              W.R. Spence, M.D., 1993

Tragedy

We can't do anything to bring people back and we can't dig people out of the freeway . . . What we can do is alter people's thought patterns for three hours—get their thoughts on something other than gloom and doom and show signs of resuming life.

      —DAVE HENDERSON,
          former major league baseball player,
          referring to playing for the Oakland Athletics after the
              earthquake that interrupted the 1989 World Series,
          as quoted in the *Washington Post*, October 20, 1989

Trash Talk

It's really getting to me. It's (trash talking) all over the league now. When you have the audacity and the nerve to talk, you better back it up. You can't talk when you're losing, when you're 11-15, because winning is what backs it up . . .

➤ RICK PITINO,
   Boston Celtics coach,
   referring to his team's propensity for trash talking,
   as quoted in the *Miami Herald*, January 9, 2000

No wonder you're all writers . . . You're terrible athletes. You're frustrated athletes, that's what you are. All of you. You can't play. You can't do nothing. And you dream all day long.

➤ MICHAEL JORDAN,
   former NBA superstar with the Chicago Bulls,
   trash-talking while playing one-on-one with sportswriter Rick
      Telander for a Sportschannel TV roundtable program called
      Sportswriters on TV

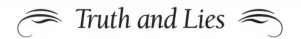

Truth and Lies

I could have easily lied. But I thought, why lie? So I told them the truth. I told them I had never eaten Wheaties and that I didn't know whether I'd even like Wheaties. I mean, we used to eat some kind of wheat puffs when I was growing up. They came in a huge bag. I don't even know if they had a brand name. We had five kids in the family. We couldn't afford Wheaties.

➤ MICHAEL JORDAN,
   former NBA superstar with the Chicago Bulls,
   when asked before signing an endorsement contract with
      Wheaties if he'd actually eaten the cereal

 *Umpires*

It's a strange business, all jeers and no cheers.

➤ Tom Gorman,
    National League umpire,
    recalled on his death,
    in the *New York Times*, August 17, 1986

Listen, Alex, on a clear day I can see the sun, and that sucker is 93 million miles away!

➤ Dick Stello,
    former major league umpire,
    when accused by Fort Worth manager Alex Grammas, while
        working in the Texas League, of not being able to see if a
        ball 250 feet away was fair or foul,
    as quoted in *Strike Two* by Ron Luciano and David Fisher,
        1984

It's the only occupation where a man has to be perfect the first day on the job and then improve over the years.

➤ Ed Runge,
    former American League umpire,
    as quoted in *Sports Illustrated*, August 20, 1973

Sometimes, although many people do not believe this, being screamed at by a manager or player standing inches away, and perhaps spitting tobacco juice on you, is not as much fun as it appears to be from a distance.

➤ Ron Luciano,
    former American League umpire,
    in *Strike Two* by Ron Luciano and David Fisher, 1984

What I really hate about umpiring is that we can never win. We don't walk off a field with a grin on our faces.

➤ Ron Luciano,
    former American League umpire,
    as quoted in *Newsweek*, September 1, 1975

The umpires have kept this game honest for 100 years. We're the only segment of the game that has never been touched by scandal. We've got to be too dumb to cheat. We must have integrity, because we sure don't have a normal family life. We certainly aren't properly paid. We have no health care, no job security, no tenure. Our pension plan is a joke. We take more abuse than any living group of humans, and can't give any back. If we're fired without notice, our only recourse is to appeal to the league president. And he's the guy that fires you. If you ask for one day off in the seven-month season, they try to make you feel three inches tall. If you call in sick, you're hounded and ostracized by the brass. Umpires must be the healthiest people on earth because none of us ever gets sick.

— RON LUCIANO,
   former American League umpire,
   a commonly cited quote

Throwing people out of a game is like learning to ride a bicycle— once you get the hang of it, it can be a lot of fun.

— RON LUCIANO,
   former American League umpire,
   as quoted in *Strike Two* by Ron Luciano and David Fisher, 1984

Let's face it, baseball is show business. Some of us take it too seriously, especially the umpires. People come out to enjoy the game, but they want a little pepper in their soup. Arguments with umpires are part of the tradition. Yet some umps are so tight they'll throw you out before you take two steps out of the dugout.

— JACK McKEON,
   longtime major league manager,
   as quoted in the *Los Angeles Herald-Examiner* February 5,
      1975, when he was manager of the Kansas City Royals

They can holler at the uniform all they want, but when they start hollering at the man wearing the uniform, they're going to be in trouble.

— JOE BRINKMAN,
   major league umpire,
   as quoted in *Strike Two* by Ron Luciano and David Fisher, 1984

Whenever you have a tight situation and there's a close pitch, the umpire gets a squawk no matter how he calls it. You wonder why men take a job in which they get so much abuse.

— RED BARBER,
legendary sportscaster, known as the "voice of the Dodgers,"
as quoted in the *New York Times*, April 25, 1976

Gentlemen, he was out . . . because I said he was out.

— BILL KLEM,
former major league umpire and member of the Baseball Hall
of Fame,
after viewing photographs that showed he'd made a bad call

I told the umpires to walk back at least 35 feet from home plate. That reduced the arguments. An angry player can't argue with the back of an umpire who is walking away.

— BILL KLEM,
former major league umpire and member of the Baseball Hall
of Fame,
giving advice to other umpires,
as quoted in *The Sporting News*, 1948

 *Violence*

Is it normal to wake up in the morning in a sweat because you can't wait to beat another human's guts out?

— JOE KAPP,
former Minnesota Vikings quarterback,
in various news summaries, December 31, 1979

Baseball, hot dogs, apple pie, and violence.

— BILL MADLOCK,
former major league baseball player,
after serving a 15-day suspension for violent behavior,
as quoted in the *Washington Post*, June 29, 1980

Baseball is a game, yes. It is also business. But what it most truly is is disguised combat. For all its gentility, its almost leisurely pace, baseball is violence under wraps.

➤ WILLIE MAYS,
   legendary Hall of Fame outfielder,
   as quoted in *Willie Mays* by Arnold Hano, 1966

Tennis is a perfect combination of violent action taking place in an atmosphere of total tranquility.

➤ BILLIE JEAN KING,
   Hall of Fame tennis player and activist for women's rights and
   **   equal pay,**
   as quoted in her book *Billie Jean*, 1982

I have always believed that a little show of force at the right time is necessary when there's a deliberate violation of law . . . I believe than when a man is involved in an overt act of violence or in destruction of someone's rights, that it's no time to conduct an experiment in education or persuasion.

➤ BRANCH RICKEY,
   president-general manager of the Brooklyn Dodgers, who
   **   brought Jackie Robinson to the Brooklyn Dodgers in 1947,**
   referring to his putting a halt to a revolt by a group of
   **   Dodgers who didn't want Robinson to play on their team,**
   as quoted in *I Never Had It Made* by Jackie Robinson, as told
   **   to Alfred Duckett, 1972**

Weather

The sky overhead is a very beautiful robin's egg blue with, as the boys say, very few angels (clouds). It's a very tough sky for the players to look into and left field in Yankee stadium is the sun garden.

➤ RED BARBER,
   legendary sportscaster, known as the "voice of the Dodgers,"
   describing field conditions during a game in one of the 13
   **   World Series that he broadcast**

Hot as Hell, ain't it Prez?

➤ BABE RUTH,
    legendary Hall of Fame outfielder,
    on being introduced to President Calvin Coolidge on a partic-
      ularly steamy day at the ballpark in Washington, D.C.,
    as quoted in *Babe: The Legend Comes to Life* by Robert W.
    Creamer, 1974

Sure holds the heat well.

➤ CASEY STENGEL,
    former manager of the New York Yankees and New York Mets,
    when asked after the 1966 All-Star Game in St. Louis, when
      the temperature hit 113 degrees on the field, how he liked
      the new St. Louis stadium

That's the first game I ever played in that had all four seasons.

➤ GLENN WILSON,
    former outfielder for the Pittsburgh Pirates,
    after playing in a game that was delayed by rain and snow,
      and finally ended in sunshine,
    as quoted in *The Sporting News,* April 24, 1989

It's a cold night out tonight. The Padres better warm up real good
because it's stiff out there.

➤ JERRY COLEMAN,
    former New York Yankees infielder and Padres announcer,
    from a collection of "Coleman-isms"

This is not a day for concerns. This is a day for pleasure. There are
concerns in baseball but they get dissolved in the bright sunshine
. . . and this is my weather. I want credit.

➤ FAY VINCENT,
    former major league baseball commissioner,
    as quoted on opening day at Shea Stadium in 1990

⇝ *Winning and Winners* ⇜

Winning isn't worthwhile unless one has something finer and nobler behind it.

➤ KNUTE ROCKNE,
former Notre Dame football coach,
while talking to Wisconsin basketball coach Walter Meanwell
during the 1920s

Winning is the science of being totally prepared.

➤ GEORGE ALLEN,
former coach of the Los Angeles Rams and Washington
Redskins, noted for his exceptional work ethic,
as quoted in *The Book of Football Wisdom*, edited by Criswell
Freeman, 1996

Everything looks nicer when you win. The girls are prettier. The cigars taste better. The trees are greener.

➤ BILLY MARTIN,
former New York Yankees player and manager,
as quoted in the *Los Angeles Times*, September 17, 1975

I have no magic formula. The only way I know to win is through hard work.

➤ DON SHULA,
legendary head coach of the Baltimore Colts and Miami
Dolphins, and the winningest coach of all-time,
as quoted in *The Book of Football Wisdom*, edited by Criswell
Freeman, 1996

When you win, you eat better, sleep better, and your beer tastes better. And your wife looks like Gina Lollabrigida.

➤ JOHNNY PESKY,
former major league baseball player and manager,
as Red Sox manager in 1963

Our good players have to step up in big games and play better. In this league, if you can't beat good teams, nothing much matters.

> ➤DANIEL SNYDER,
> Washington Redskins owner,
> discussing his expectations for the team,
> as quoted in *Sports Illustrated*, November 15, 1999

Before you can win a game, you have to not lose it.

> ➤CHUCK NOLL,
> former coach of the Pittsburgh Steelers,
> as quoted in *Get Lost Adventure Magazine*

Close games make me nervous.

> ➤COLONEL JACOB RUPPERT,
> owner of the New York Yankees from 1915 to 1939,
> referring to why he liked his team to win at least 10-0

Boys, baseball is a game where you gotta have fun. You do that by winning.

> ➤DAVE BRISTOL,
> manager of the Cincinnati Reds,
> on becoming the Reds manager,
> as quoted in *Time*, May 26, 1967

I'm only interested in winning ballgames and I can't be worrying about whether the sun's out or the moon's out.

> ➤JIM FREY,
> former Chicago Cubs manager,
> on the controversy over night baseball,
> as quoted in the *New York Times*, June 17, 1985

I never did say that you can't be a nice guy and win. I said that if I was playing third base and my mother rounded third with the winning run, I'd trip her up.

> ➤LEO DUROCHER,
> former Hall of Fame manager of the Brooklyn Dodgers and
> New York Giants,
> in *The Speaker's Electronic Reference Collection*, AApex
> Software, 1994

Winning isn't everything, it's the only thing.

> ← Vince Lombardi,
> **legendary former coach of the Green Bay Packers and
> Washington Redskins,
> widely attributed**

When you win, nothing hurts.

> ← Joe Namath,
> **Hall of Fame quarterback,
> as quoted in *The Guinness Dictionary of Sports Quotations*
> by Colin Jarman, 1990**

Winning is everything. The only ones who remember you when you come second are your wife and your dog.

> ← Damon Hill,
> **English race car driver
> as quoted in the *Sunday Times* Quotes of the Year, December
> 18, 1994**

Winning isn't everything, but wanting to is.

> ← Arnold Palmer,
> **Hall of Fame golfer,
> as quoted in *The Guinness Dictionary of Sports Quotations*
> by Colin Jarman, 1990**

A winner never stops trying.

> ← Tom Landry,
> **legendary former coach of the Dallas Cowboys,
> from *The Ultimate Success Quotations Library*, Cyber Nation
> International, Inc., Reno, NV, 1997**

You've got to win in sports—that's talent—but you've also got to learn how to remind everybody how you did win, and how often. That comes with experience.

> ← Billie Jean King,
> **Hall of Fame tennis player and activist for women's rights and
> equal pay,
> from her book *Billie Jean*, 1982**

In sports, you simply aren't considered a real champion until you have defended your title successfully. Winning it once can be a fluke; winning it twice proves that you are the best.

➤ALTHEA GIBSON,
Hall of Fame tennis player and the first African-American player to win the U.S. Open and Wimbledon championships,
from her book *I Always Wanted to Be Somebody*, 1958

A tie is like kissing your sister.

➤DUFFY DAUGHERTY,
head football coach at Michigan State,
as quoted in the *The Book of Football Wisdom*, edited by Criswell Freeman, 1996

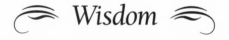

Wisdom

Some coaches pray for wisdom. I pray for 260-pound tackles. They'll give me plenty of wisdom.

➤CHUCK NOLL,
former head coach of the Pittsburgh Steelers,
as quoted in *The Book of Football Wisdom*, edited by Criswell Freeman, 1996

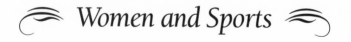

Women and Sports

I think the key is for women not to set any limits.

➤MARTINA NAVRATILOVA,
Hall of Fame tennis player,
as quoted in *Words of Women: Quotations for Success* by Power Dynamics Publishing, 1997

Will we ever see another Babe? Certainly we will, in time, and maybe we have one in our midst now. Does anyone doubt that Jackie Joyner-Kersee might be a big-league prospect if she had concentrated on baseball? And with a ballplayer having broken the $3 million-a-year salary barrier, won't the extraordinary women athlete be tempted to go for it? . . . We will see a woman in the majors before we see one in the NBA or NFL, and when it happens—not *if* it happens— it will excite the masses like nothing we have ever seen in sports. If you can remember the furor over Billie Jean King and Bobby Riggs' tennis battle of the sexes [in 1973]. . . you can imagine how big this one will be.

➤ BILL TANTON,
sportswriter,
in a column in the *Baltimore Evening Sun* in 1989

It's cutting edge. Who wouldn't want to be pioneering for women's athletics? We're part of history.

➤ SHANNON DAVIS,
quarterback of the Women's Professional Football League's
Minnesota Vixens,
referring to her decision to join the fledgling league,
as quoted in *Sports Illustrated*, October 11, 1999

I think I can say with safety that woman's championship golf has not only come to stay, but that it's sure to keep growing all the way from here on in.

➤ NANCY LOPEZ,
Hall of Fame golfer,
as quoted in *Golfers on Golf*, edited by Downs MacRury, 1997

This will be the world's premier league for women's soccer. One of the things we realized and have known for a while is how deep the player pool is. The level of competition is going to be extremely high.

➤ MIA HAMM,
a star with the U.S. women's World Cup champions,
referring to the newly formed Women's United Soccer
Association,
as quoted on *ESPNet SportsZone*

People feel there is something very attractive and enduring that these women (the U.S. World Cup soccer team) have touched deep within the fabric of American society—it's not just soccer moms, it's soccer dads and soccer uncles. The consensus was that the ideal time to consider the launch of the league would be after the 1999 World Cup. We think this is an exciting time; we think we have the right ingredients.

➤ JOHN HENDRICKS,
founder of the Discovery Channel and the force behind the
Women's United Soccer Association,
referring to the formation of the league,
as quoted on *ESPNet SportsZone*

When we complain about conditions, we're just bitches. But when the men complain, people think, "Well, it really must be hard."

➤ BETSY KING,
Hall of Fame golfer,
as quoted on *Golfers on Golf*, edited by Downs MacRury, 1997

≈ Index ≈

About the Editors

Mike McGovern is an assistant sports editor and columnist for the *Reading* (Pa.) *Eagle-Times*.

Susan Shelly is a freelance writer and researcher. A former newspaper reporter and columnist, she's written more than a dozen books. They have two children, Sara and Ryan McGovern, and live in Shillington, PA.